# Freedom: Promise and Menace

*A Critique on the Cult of Freedom*

by SCOTT NEARING

Social Science Institute
Harborside, Maine

PRINTED IN U.S.A.

1

## PREFACE

During the past decade the manuscript of this book has undergone a series of revolutionary transformations. Never in the course of a piece of social research have I changed my assumptions so fundamentally and so often. The theme grew out of a study of the social crisis which has dominated and conditioned the centers of western civilization for more than half a century. While thumbing through and sorting out the available material on the period I found the word "freedom" cropping up with increasing frequency. The more I read, heard and considered, the more evident it became that the freedom concept was playing a major theoretical and political role in crystallizing opinion and popularizing policy.

Changing times are swelling the ranks of the freedom devotees. Freedom is being widely used by a variety of people in many and diverse connections. In the social transformation symbolized by the American-French revolutions "liberty" was the slogan of the revolutionaries; whereas in the present world crisis conservatives are using the "freedom" slogan to win support for their reactionary policies. The word "freedom" is being used so loosely and

iii

indiscriminately that it has lost any specific meaning and become a source of misunderstanding and confusion.

Much has been written about freedom in recent years. Students of social problems in all parts of the world have done research, discussed, and published books, pamphlets and articles on freedom, its problems and possibilities. My reason for adding to this flood of freedom literature is that I am not a freedom advocate but an analyst of its nature and consequences. I have tried in this study to separate the freedom concept from political oratory; to emancipate it from the corrupting influence of emotional patrioteers and sentimental liberals; to discuss its sociological background and its organic place in the life of power age individuals and social groups.

Personally I have gained a great deal from this intensive study of freedom. Except for the war years from 1915-1918, I have not learned so much in so short a time. I hope that other students of social science will use the results of this study. Be that as it may, I am grateful for the opportunity to make the study, to formulate its conclusions, and to add one more volume to the series of Social Science Handbooks published by the Social Science Institute.

SCOTT NEARING

June 30, 1961

# TABLE OF CONTENTS

## III. *THE FREEDOM—RESTRAINT OPPOSITION*

## IV. *THE ROLE OF FREEDOM AND RESTRAINT IN THE POWER AGE*

*Part I*

# Freedom as Idea

# 1. WHAT IS FREEDOM?

Freedom and such associated ideas as liberty, independence and self-determination have been examined and discussed for at least twenty-five centuries. Lord Acton, in his *Essays on Freedom and Power,* noted that the stoics urged their hearers to discover the principles "that ought to regulate the lives of men and the existence of society," thereby laying the foundations for many subsequent examinations of freedom in theory and practice. Great changes have taken place in the use and meaning of freedom since the days when Aristotle argued that chattel slavery and war were among the indispensable foundations of freedom for the elite.

Any review of the age-old discussions regarding the meaning and significance of freedom should begin with a clarification of viewpoint and a re-sorting of subject matter, since philosophers, theologians and social scientists have spoken and written on the theme without arriving at exact definitions. Verbal misunderstandings, scientific, technical, psychological and theological, dot the history of human inquiry and exposition. If words were used precisely, the chances for enlightenment and agreement would

3

be greatly increased. Precision is particularly important in dealing with generalized ideas and concepts such as freedom.

Where there are wide differences in approach and classification, it seems essential for each participant in a discussion to define his terms and, if possible, to abide by the definitions throughout his presentation. Particularly in a relatively new field, such as the sociology of freedom, exactness in language should be a major consideration.

In the course of my reading I have jotted down several score definitions of freedom, covering a wide range of thought and outlook. We must be content to select a few representative examples of those many definitions.

Most writers and thinkers have regarded freedom as the attitude of a man toward his work, his life and his environment. Immanuel Kant, in his *Philosophy of Law,* used freedom to mean independence of the compulsory will of another, in so far as this does not interfere with the general freedom. Another oft-repeated definition is that freedom involves getting rid of restriction or restraint. More specifically, Lyman Bryson in *Science and Freedom*[1] believes that freedom is a result of having a sufficient number and variety of choices to make changes and diversify life. Walton H. Hamilton describes freedom as an opportunity for man to make the most of himself.[2] Plato, Spinoza and other philosophers identified freedom with the attainment of a level of wisdom that places man beyond the bondage to desire. Confucius and his many disciples sought freedom by following the Golden Mean.

American and English liberal thinking associates freedom with individualism—the success of a person in being himself, especially his rational self. Freedom, they think, comes with the elimination or reduction of impediments. Harold Laski listed three essentials of freedom: a harmonious balance of the personality, the absence of restraint, and opportunity to exercise initiative.[3] Horace Kallen considers freedom not as a positive force but a negative one,—a removal of religious, civil, personal and political obstruction or interference with thought and action.[4] Richard McKeon holds that freedom permits the individual to act according to his own nature; freedom being opposed to restraints imposed by external causes.[5] Louis Le Fevre finds freedom where the individual is not subject to restraint or control by others, except by an authority and for a purpose which the restrained person recognizes as legitimate.[6] John MacMurray holds that freedom means spontaneity. It is doing what we want to do without constraint, either in us or outside us.[7]

Finally, Mortimer Adler, in his book *The Idea of Freedom*,[8] after elaborating a logician's theory of freedom, gives an abbreviated definition "acceptable to common sense." His commonsense definition is in three parts: A man is free if he can choose the course he wishes to follow; if he is able to carry out his decision in action, and if he is in a position to achieve the objectives of his choice.

These examples suggest the variety, diversity and conflict of the meanings which various thinkers and writers have attached to the freedom concept. They serve to emphasize the difficulties faced by anyone who is anxious to achieve exactness of meaning in this very important field of thought.

Dictionary definitions of freedom are reasonably uniform, though they cover a wide territory. In Funk and Wagnall's *New Standard Dictionary* "free" means: "1. Not bound by restrictions, physical, governmental, or moral, and whether as respects one's views, desires, inclinations or conduct: exempt from arbitrary domination or direction; not subject to the control of external force or authority; at liberty; independent." "2. *Ethics* Self-determining . . . possessed of so-called free will." "3. *Political* Having political liberty . . . as a free nation." "4. Liberated by reason of age . . . at 21 a man is free." "5. Enjoying certain immunities . . . as freedom of the city." "6. Exempt from, . . . as free from pain." 7. Informal, unconventional. 8. Forward; impertinent; indelicate; careless, reckless. 9. Unrestrained, unimpeded, "as a free channel." 10. Without restriction or cost, "as free seats." 11. Liberal, generous, "as free with money." 12. Not closely bound by pattern, "as a free sketch." 13. Not attached or bound, "as the free end of a rope." Nearly half a page is devoted to the multiple meanings of free. Freedom is defined as "the state or condition of being free: liberty, independence, immunity, exemption."

Most of these variations of meaning have no direct relation to the sociology of freedom. They are given here because they are indicative of the range of meanings attached to the freedom concept.

Roget's *Dictionary of Synonyms and Antonyms* devotes an entire page to the synonyms of freedom. Among the nouns given as synonyms are the following, in order listed: liberty, independence, emancipation, liberation, release, manumission, enlargement, immunity, enfranchisement, exemption, franchise, privilege, prerogative, right. Other synonyms are grouped under: scope, frankness, ease, boldness, familiarity, license, autonomy, freeman, independent. Beside the nouns, Roget lists verbs, adjectives and adverbs which are related to the freedom concept.

Three aspects of these definitions are noteworthy. Freedom is associated chiefly with the individual observer and definer; it is not a good in itself, but is frequently related to an opposite such as restraint. This general emphasis on the individual as observer, thinker, planner and beneficiary of freedom justifies a new study which centers around freedom as an aspect of association.

An analysis of the meaning of freedom is summarized in the definition which will be used throughout this study. Freedom is opportunity to make choices and decisions and to translate them into action,—unrestricted, uncoerced, independent, sovereign. Freedom requires self-determination, whether the involved entity be an individual or a social group. Freedom exists when the individual or social group has an unrestricted opportunity for self expression,—physically, emotionally, mentally, spiritually. This is a positive, constructive and creative concept.

Freedom is a resultant of equilibrium and normal function, of health or wholth, individual or social. Freedom is a chance to be and to become. Freedom is not monolithic, but multiple. It includes the physical, emotional, intellectual and spiritual life of the individual. Likewise it includes the local group—family, neighborhood and the larger group—city, state, nation, world community.

## 2. FREEDOM IMPLIES SEPARATENESS

Perhaps the most obvious aspect of the freedom idea is its separatist character. Freedom implies separateness,—including preparations for division or departure, the actual process of separation, and the subsequent independence which results from separation.

If the first question confronting a human being is "to be or not to be"; the second question is "to belong or not to belong." Belonging means attachment. Freedom means detachment. Those who are attached go along together. Those who detach go their own separate ways. The implications of separateness are present in the life of each individual and of each group and sub-group composing the human race.

From birth (which involves separation from the mother) the individual human is confronted by a dilemma,—to remain as close as possible to the mother or to break away, separate himself from the mother and strike out on his own account. If he remains close to the mother he enjoys the security of comfort, companionship and love. If he breaks away, he enjoys the thrill of initiating, adventuring, experimenting.

Again and again as the individual matures he is confronted by the same dilemma, the security of the "We" or the freedom of the "I",—group solidarity versus individual initiative. It is possible to deal with this dilemma by saying "Why choose? Let us have both." Human beings, except the most solitary, do have a certain amount of "I-ness" and of "We-ness" all through their lives. A Confucian Golden Mean implies a course between the extremes. At certain points, however, such as birth, choosing a profession and mate, leaving the parental roof, establishing a home, having children, becoming a citizen, joining voluntary associations, choices must be made.

Forces, working ceaselessly in opposite directions, attract and repel. Attraction brings together or unites. Repulsion separates or fragments. In certain cases these forces are referred to as centriputal and centrifugal. They operate in society as well as in nature.

Early in life individuals and communities learn the advantages which come from togetherness. Indeed, the human infant has little choice in the matter. At birth he is so nearly helpless that in the absence of attention and care he would perish from hunger and exposure to the elements.

Equally, by taking part in social activities, men learn that by participating in common tasks or through specialization, division of labor and the exchange of goods and services they can amplify and multiply the advantages which come from utilizing nature and providing communally shared social services. The rewards of collective effort are manifest. The dangers of separation from the group are manifold.

Growing toward maturity the individual cannot escape group pressures, no matter how he may resent them. The group or community of which he is part attracts by its offers of security, convenience and comfort while it repels by the conformities and responsibilities which group life necessarily imposes.

Emphasis on freedom separates the individual from the group and even sets the individual against the group, urging him to pursue his own interests even though such conduct may disrupt or damage the group of which he is a member and to which he feels certain loyalties. Self-determining and atomistic, the urge to freedom puts the part before the whole, as it stretches or breaks the bonds that hold the individual within the group.

A group composed of individuals is a whole, made up of functioning, interdependent parts. A drop of water seems to merge with other drops, losing its individuality in the totality of the pool or stream or sea. In the case of human beings, such complete merging in the group is unlikely or impossible. Each human being is an individual—a coordinated, integrated organism, which does not and cannot merge with other humans, though it may join them and identify itself with them. While life remains, the human "I" persists. Each expression of "I-ness" distinguishes and, to a degree, separates the "I" from the "We."

Since each individual is a self-conscious, unique being, differing in some respects from all other members of his group, each has qualities, capacities and interests different from those of his fellows. As a member of the group, he shares common interests. As an individual he has special interests. Even where special interests do not contradict or obstruct group interests, they take individual attention away from the group and thus weaken collective purpose and collective action.

Freedom to pursue individual interests at the expense of the common interests may undermine and threaten the common welfare. Carried to the extreme of dismemberment, the pursuit of individual interests impairs, disrupts and perhaps destroys the group.

Freedom, by stressing particular interests at the expense of the general welfare, distinguishes, separates and finally detaches the freedom-seeker from the group. The seeker after freedom is first of all an individual following the call of his own interests. He may be an inventor, painter, poet, botanist, responding to the urges of his native genius. Presumably he is more creative than many of his contemporaries. Under the impetus of his talent, he blazes his own path through unexplored country, leaving his fellows far behind. If he ever had an abiding interest in the general welfare, he has ignored it or deliberately by-passed it in his search for the objectives of his particular goal.

Seeking after individual goals may lead, as one of its earliest consequences, to an avoidance of social responsibility. At best, the talented human being must weigh the call of his genius against the call to civic duty. At worst, he rushes forward along his chosen path without giving more than a passing thought to his fellow citizens or considering their feelings or concerns. In most cases however the freedom-seeker is torn by the contradictions between the pursuit of his personal interests and his feelings of group solidarity and responsibility.

Freedom for the individual to go his own way, at his own pace, separates him from the group. Further, it makes him stand out above the group, and perhaps beyond it. No longer is he an indistinguishable member of an undifferentiated herd or mass.

Rather, he has moved out of the community and probably away from it. Often, in an emergency, such an act may provide the community with leadership. If the group responds to the initiative, the deviant becomes a group leader. If his leadership proves successful, community life follows the new pattern, recognizing and acclaiming its new leader as a community benefactor.

Usually, however, events follow a different course. Long-established community patterns, with their consequent habit complexes, have enmeshed the members of the community so completely that they are unable to change, resent change, and resist it if it is forced upon them.

Furthermore, the one who has broken away from the established group pattern has distinguished himself and thus set himself up as an example for others. Thus he challenges his fellows to follow the new path which he has blazed, while they challenge him, calling upon him to return to the established ways. Tension grows. Conflict ensues. The group divides into the radicals who accept and adopt the new ideas and techniques and the conservatives who insist upon preserving the established culture pattern.

Such a conflict may lead to a split in community life, with the radicals declaring their independence and going off on their own. Or it may end in the defeat and dissolution of the radicals and the restoration of the status quo. Or the radicals may be strong enough to take over the leadership of the community and inaugurate a new life pattern. If not too deep or too long-established, the rift may end in negotiation and compromise.

Demands for freedom challenge the established order. Even in instances where freedom is assured under law, the freedom-seekers meet stubborn resistance from upholders of the status quo. Habit patterns and vested interests join hands to preserve the status quo and do their utmost (by law where feasible or by force and violence when necessary) to preserve and perpetuate existing institutions.

The divisive nature of freedom-demands appears most clearly when one segment of a community seeks to advance its interests at the expense of other segments or in opposition to their insistence upon preserving the established order. Power-seizure and civil war are frequent outcomes of such situations.

Rival groups in free enterprise economies may advance claims. Where no solution can be found that is acceptable to both sides, civil strife ensues. It may be the mild strife incident to a strike or lock-out, with labor on one side and management on the other. It may take the form of an armed conflict like recent civil wars in Spain and China. It may result in the rebellion of colonial peoples against their imperial overlords, involving large scale military operations. Finally, such a conflict may lead into social revolution. Recent history provides numerous examples of all of these possibilities in the activities of free enterprise economies and free, or sovereign, political states.

Whether examples are chosen from the relations between communities and the freedom-seekers among their members, or the rivalries between organized groups within a community, or the competition between communities seeking to advance themselves at the expense of neighbor groups, the outcome is the same. The freedom idea is separatist. It involves separation, leads quickly to competition, and frequently into conflict. Freedom demands are divisive and fragmentive forces. Freedom for the individual or the group implies and involves deviation, division, separation.

## 3. FREEDOM AS RELATIONSHIP

The segment of the universe in which we live and with which we are best acquainted consists of relationships. Perhaps it would be more correct to say that from the minute to the immense, from the atom to the solar system, attributes or parts are integrated or built into wholes or totalities. Microscope, telescope and spectroscope supplement our senses in reporting relationships, similarities and differences throughout the parts of the manifested universe that come under our observation.

Polarity (or the principle of opposites) appears in nature, in society and in the life experiences of each individual. Positive and negative electric charges have a current or arc between them. The north pole is on one side of the planet; the south pole on the other, with the earth between. Life experience is favorable or unfavorable, pleasant or painful, plus or minus. All of these terms: positive-negative, north-south, favorable-unfavorable, pleasant-painful, describe relationships between opposites.

Under these conditions it is impossible to consider any observation or any experience entirely by itself, because no thought or thing exists by itself. Within its own borders it is an actuality or entity; at its borders it touches other entities. Together, aggregates of entities constitute other wholes of greater magnitude. Relationship, grouping, association are among the essential features of manifestation, of being, of reality.

Relationships, groupings and associations are not random. If an element of randomness exists, it is the exception rather than the rule. Relationships, at the least, are balanced and sequential. At the maximum they are purposed and directed. When relationships are disturbed or upset by the intrusion of external forces, another balance or equilibrium between divergent forces is sought and eventually established. Balance, or equilibrium, exists in human society as in other areas such as physics, chemistry and mechanics. In social relations as elsewhere, balance or equilibrium exists between related forces.

The idea of freedom is no exception to this general principle. Freedom does not exist by itself, in a vacuum, but in association with one or more related ideas. We have described freedom as divisive or separational. Separateness, in one sense, is negative. Separation means breaking up of established relationships, or breaking away from existing situations. To separate is to divide, disunite, sever. In the process of separation a pre-existing unity is brought to an end by an act which is not only divisive but destructive.

Freedom may arise out of negation or destruction, but it is more than either. Like other ideas, freedom does not stand alone. It is associated with ideas which are alike (and which may be complementary) and with other ideas which are dissimilar. Some of these dissimilar ideas are opposed or opposite to the idea of freedom. As it is impossible to think of positive without negative, of north without south, of advantageous without disadvantageous, it is likewise impossible to think of freedom without its associates —some of which are its opposites.

Harold Laski in his *Liberty in the Modern State* sums up the relation in one sentence: "Liberty is essentially an absence of restraint." Consequently, freedom in the power age is "a purely negative condition."[9] Horace Kallen amplifies this idea of the negative aspects of freedom: "No political or social scientist has yet produced, so far as I know, a description of freedom as a positive, intrinsic quality of the course of nature or the life of man. . . . Freedom seems . . . to require the presence of its opposites and enemies in order to experience its intrinsic character."[10]

Since freedom has various meanings and is used in different connections it has several opposites: such as restraint, control, interference, intervention, regulation, compulsion, coercion. Each of these ideas is associated with freedom: freedom-restraint, freedom-interference, freedom-regulation, freedom-coercion.

For the purposes of this discussion let us use the relationship of freedom-restraint: first, because it is simple and easily understood; second, because it is recognized in most discussions of the subject; and third, because it is general rather than specific. Later in our presentation we shall contrast freedom and obligation (rights-duties), also freedom-responsibility, a negative-positive confrontation. The rights-duties opposition is commonly used in discussions of good citizenship. Our choice of freedom-restraint is based on typicality and convenience. It is not intended to be in any sense exclusive. One or another of the freedom opposites would serve our purposes almost equally.

Action, function, change and development in the lives of individuals and communities take place between the poles of opposing forces. Imagine a line drawn across this page. The left end of the line is labeled "freedom," the right end labeled "restraint." The line is divided into twenty-one parts. The part at the left is numbered "freedom 20—restraint 0." The part at the right is numbered "freedom 0—restraint 20." At the center is a point labeled "freedom 10—restraint 10." Each point on the line represents a different degree or mixture of freedom-restraint. On the left of the line freedom predominates, while restraint is subordinate, reaching zero at the extreme left. At the other end of the line restraint predominates, with freedom reaching zero at the extreme right. The ends of the line are two affirmations: one of complete freedom, the other of complete restraint. These affirmations and the various stations along the line constitute an associational complex of varying degrees of relationship between the opposing ideas or forces.

The freedom-restraint opposition exists in the following instance. An obdurate parent says: "I have a right to my own children. I will keep them at home and will not send them to school." Society answers: "All children are members of the community. We have decided that it is in the best interests of the community that all of its members should have a formal education. To insure the general welfare we have passed a compulsory education law requiring all children from 6 to 15 to attend school. Under this law you as a parent have no choice. You *must* send your children to school."

The individual demands freedom to go his own way. The community requires a degree of conformity sufficient to ensure the general welfare. In practice when two such affirmations have been made, there is a gap between the two positions. This gap is a field for discussion, negotiation, and possible agreement or of misunderstanding, hostility, tension and conflict.

Group projects and actions, like the projects and actions of individuals, follow courses that range somewhere between the freedom-restraint poles. They shift and change with the course of events. There is no permanent relationship between freedom-restraint, nor is there a lasting dominant direction in human affairs toward greater freedom or toward greater restraint. The proportions of freedom-restraint at any given place and time seem to be determined by the momentum of trends and the interaction of established social forces or the introduction of new forces at particular times and under particular circumstances.

United States experience has been noteworthy in this respect. After the middle of the 18th century, British governmental restrictions on American colonial trade led to a split in the ranks of the colonists. Colonial conservatives upheld Britain's right to levy taxes. Republicans demanded freedom from British monarchical restrictions. The ensuing conflict led to the establishment in the former colonies of economic enterprise free from government restriction. After the War of 1812, when it became evident that many U.S.A. free enterprises would be ruined by the dumping of British and other European manufactures on the American market, the advocates of free enterprise asked and obtained government intervention and subsidy in the form of protective tariffs. Subsequent struggles for the domestic market convinced U.S.A. free enterprisers that larger profits could be made by combination than under competition. The resulting consolidations of railroads and other business enterprises led to congressional acts forbidding restraint of interstate commerce. Throughout the century from 1815 to 1914 the policies and actions of U.S.A. economy moved back and forth between laissez-faire on one side and government intervention and regulation on the other.

On the whole, the course of events during this century has led the United States economy away from freedom toward restraint. Inside the business world, little businesses have been replaced by big business combinations and consolidations, while government regulation of the economy has broadened and deepened. The pattern has taken several forms,—the planned, ordered sequence of business consolidation; the "thou shalt not" of government limitations on trust organization, and the "thou shalt" implicit in government tax programs.

Social movement is not necessarily from the small to the large and from the simple to the complex. For three centuries British and French empire builders extended their controls over geographic areas and peoples in the Americas, Asia and Africa until a half dozen imperial centers in western and central Europe held substantial economic and political power over large portions of the planet. In terms of our discussion, European imperialists were determining the economic and political affairs of large numbers of peoples living in the Asian-African colonies. After 1910 a reverse process set in and the demand for freedom and self-determination resulted in the dismemberment of the European empires and the formation of numerous independent nations from the fragments of the former empires. Even at this early stage it is evident that the newly liberated colonial peoples are establishing groupings, alliances, federations in the same way as the thirteen British colonies of North America organized first a confederation and later a federation under a central government.

Two conclusions grow out of our analysis. One is that freedom as an idea cannot be considered by itself because it is always associated with other ideas, some of which are opposites of freedom. The second conclusion is that the relationship between two opposing ideas such as freedom and restraint is constantly changing. These changes lead to alterations in the balance, which tips now toward freedom and again toward restraint, yielding to situations in which freedom increases at the expense of restraint or restraint increases at the expense of freedom.

## 4.  FREEDOM AS CAUSE

Freedom advocates consider freedom a first cause of human well-being. The most enthusiastic among them go so far as to insist that freedom is *the* first cause. "The very perception of Being depends upon freedom, which is itself prior to Being."[11] They formulate this faith in the slogan: Freedom Comes First.

Struggles to be free, and the exercise of freedoms once obtained, have been among the major factors in the development of western civilization. Classical economists and advocates of the free enterprise system contended that private ownership would lead the free-holder to turn a desert into a garden, while a leasehold would incline the tenant to convert a garden into a desert.

Without doubt, economic free enterprise has played an important and decisive role in developing a culture pattern that has broadly increased man's control over many aspects of nature, that has added to his understanding of social forces and his ability to manipulate them and that has greatly increased man's knowledge of the intricacies and possibilities of human nature. We can go further and agree with the freedom advocates that the liberation from medieval restraints known as the rebirth or renaissance of southern and western Europe stimulated the creative genius of Italians, Dutch, French and British artists and writers, and was directly responsible for the flowering of pictorial art, architecture, poetry, drama.

Many causes operate at various levels in every complex social situation. While it is not possible to estimate with any accuracy the precise contribution made by any causative factor to a general social up-swing like the European Renaissance, there can be no question but that the lifting of feudal restrictions and the opening of new avenues to advancement and achievement under bourgeois auspices were factors which played a prominent role in determining the course taken by European society during the subsequent period.

Lester F. Ward's *Applied Sociology* is a collection of material brought together to illustrate the role played by enlarged opportunity in providing outlets for creative human capacities. Heretofore, Professor Ward argued, the talent and genius which expressed themselves in present-day culture have been drawn from about one-tenth of the population,—the tenth that has been freed from the day-to-day struggle to provide the bare necessities. Liberate man from the food struggle, he asserted, and you multiply by ten the volume of human capacity available for dealing with the problems, utilizing the opportunities and making the improvements now easily attainable in stabilizing and ordering human society.

From an entirely different field comes a parallel contention. Dr. Henry E. Sigerist, in *Disease and Civilization*[12] noted the prevalence of ill-health among humans. What is the cause of these disease-limitations on living normal, vital lives? Dr. Sigerist answered with one word—"poverty." Where poverty has been eliminated, human health has been improved and human life prolonged.

From still another field, Professor Paul A. Baran writes in *The Political Economy of Growth*[13] that two-thirds of mankind are victims of backwardness, insufficient and inadequate food, physical ailments, illnesses, defects, ignorance, prejudice, superstition. This sad state of affairs exists because of lack of the economic surpluses needed to provide the equipment required for production, distribution, sanitation, education. As these backward areas are liberated from the restrictions of colonialism, and as they secure adequate capital, they can rebuild their own culture patterns, raising themselves by their bootstraps to higher social levels. Human society can be liberated from general backwardness as it can be liberated from poverty when capital goods and technical know-how are made available in areas of restricted opportunity.

We are living through an era of rapid, drastic changes in the culture pattern of western civilization. Important economic, political and social transformations are taking place in a single generation, as in the Soviet Union after 1917; in a single decade, as in China after 1949; in a single year as in Cuba after January 1, 1959. One of the characteristic aspects of these revolutionary developments is the widespread sense of emancipation from outmoded, out-worn social institutions and procedures. Dormant, static, oppressed, exploited masses of people throw off the restraints and limitations of the past and in a burst of energy and enthusiasm attack the problems of organizing and building a new and better social pattern. Such developments, which have become commonplace in the revolutionary situations of the past half-century, justify Lester Ward's contention that opening the gates of opportunity multiplies social achievement by releasing funds of pent-up energy.

Devotees of freedom have urged its importance as an incentive to progress. It was the freedom of 15th century free-booters to voyage, discover, expropriate and exploit which touched off the Europeanization of the planet after 1450. It was freedom from land monopoly, hereditary aristocracy and feudal restraints on trade and commerce that led to the speedy industrialization and modernization of the Americas and Australasia by white Europeans.

There can be no question concerning the stimulating effect of the "get-rich-quick" appeal in galvanizing average humans into action during recent times in lands opened to European settlement. The history of the North American frontier from 1700 to 1900 must convince the most sceptical that freedom to occupy and exploit, on the gambler's chance of easy-come-money, has proved to be not only a stimulus but an intoxicant of extreme potency.

In these and other instances enlarging the areas of choice, making decisions, and embodying these decisions in action have proved to be causative, moving forces of immense significance, fraught with noteworthy possibilities.

Having recognized the importance of the freedom urge as a social force and having cited some of the many advantageous results that have been derived from a shift in the life pattern away from restraint and toward freedom, a somewhat different note should be introduced into this phase of the discussion. The enlargement of opportunity and the consequent increase in freedom have their shadows as well as their lights.

Freedom has been treated by its advocates as an unmixed blessing. "Make us free," they have urged, "so that we may enjoy the good things of life." Is this assumption borne out by experience? Does freedom lead necessarily to survival, to security and happiness?

Freedom and restraint have stood at opposite poles of the social balance for ages. What does history have to report concerning the causal relation between freedom, survival, security and happiness? The answer can be stated in two simple propositions. First, social history is a record of restraints rather than freedoms. One civilization after another has amassed wealth and augmented its power. As it has matured it has multiplied restraints without corresponding increases in freedom. During the earlier phases of the cycles of civilization freedom has been more in evidence. As civilizations grow in wealth, population, complexity and overhead costs, restraints have been imposed, not only upon public business, but upon private affairs. In one civilization after another, maturity has led to the multiplication of restrictions.

By the end of the 19th century when western civilization had reached the pinnacle of its wealth and power, feudal restraints had been replaced by a multiplicity of legal controls over the lives of citizens. Today, in the name of freedom, new restraints are hedging in the lives of individuals and communities.

There are no clear proofs that a shift of private or public life away from restraint toward freedom will better the chances of survival or augment security or happiness. Through frequent repetitions of their slogans, freedom advocates have popularized their cause and won temporary support from substantial constituencies. In the long run, however, majority consent and approval have supported an emphasis on restraint rather than freedom. While freedom has frequently enjoyed temporary popularity, the need for security and survival have led not to an enlargement of freedoms but to a search for more adequate restraints. Freedom, in a word, may be self-defeating. Its exercise may produce results quite different from those anticipated and intended by its advocates.

Freedom is not a constant or dependable cause of well-being. There are times when individuals and communities seek their welfare by enlarging freedom. At other times the demand for restraints exceeds the demand for freedom. At times freedom leads to enlarged opportunities. At other times the exercise of freedoms leads to restrictions and restraints. There is no simple, reliable formula such as "with increasing freedom comes greater happiness and well-being." More freedom is not of itself a cause of greater benefits and satisfactions for more people.

## 5. FREEDOM AS CONSEQUENCE

Freedom has been one of the causes leading to the development of power age society. It is also one of the consequences of that development.

Freedom in the power age is not derived from nature. On the contrary, nature seems to be restrained and patterned with little more than narrow margins for variation or deviation. Beyond those margins, variants and deviants are cut off by the pitiless action of natural selection. Nature's patterns, once established, are followed more or less consistently. The whole dominates its parts and keeps them functioning in their appointed places. The general takes precedence over the particular. Nature, on the whole, is not free, but patterned.

There is little evidence that the love of freedom is inherent in human nature. Most human beings through most of recorded history have lived as slaves, serfs, vassals or tenants, obeying not their own urges but the will of their owners and masters. If to the bonds of mastery we add those of tradition, custom and habit, most human beings are bound, not free. John Dewey, in his *Freedom and Culture*[14] points out that the population of the United States, which was rural and agricultural in the days of Thomas Jefferson, had become urban and industrial in the days of Thomas A. Edison. This transformation in the life pattern of an entire people has been accepted with little more than a ripple of protest from a few cranks and faddists. Human nature adjusted itself to the new way of life because human beings readily adopt and conform with only occasional question, resentment or resistance. Humanity prefers comfort and convenience to struggle and freedom.

Arguments are advanced to show that certain freedoms are based on "natural" rights. The right to go and come, for example, is often called "natural": man being able to move about on land with his biological equipment, feet and legs. Movement in the power age, on land, on water, in the air and in space is based not upon man's natural heritage but on his social achievements and arrangements.

Freedom, a man-made product, is the consequence of the efforts made by social groups to broaden opportunity for their members. Anyone is free to go by train or plane from New York City to Chicago, so long as he complies with the rules and holds a ticket. But this freedom is based not on nature (and not on human nature) but on the efforts of society. The two cities are separated by a thousand miles. To cover this distance in a few hours involves the construction of facilities—rail lines, stations, airports, trains and planes, supplied with fuel and manned by trained crews. In preparation for such a trip great numbers of individuals have performed essential preliminary tasks. The sum total of these collective efforts makes possible a quick and safe journey from New York to Chicago. The freedom to make this trip is a consequence of specialized, interdependent, responsible group action. Society provided this freedom, and can abrogate it. Freedom to move, except on foot or animal back, is largely a consequence of social organization and action.

Man's freedom in the power age is in large measure a consequence of group plans, arrangements, activities. First there are the cultural traits and patterns developed through generations. Second, each generation must provide the facilities and the trained personnel necessary for the establishment and maintenance of the educational apparatus. Freedoms currently enjoyed by individuals and social groups do not come from nature. On the contrary, they are the outcome of purposive individual and group know-how, coordination and function.

This view is widely held among thinkers and writers on freedom. Acton described liberty as "the delicate fruit of a mature civilization."[15] Harold Laski argues that freedom is the outcome of social conditions, especially of the educational system and state intervention in the affairs of its citizens.[16] Herbert J. Miller states that freedom is a product of social and cultural traditions, arrangements and practices.[17]

Freedom is a product of group organization and activity,—a

social product. It is also the result of struggle within the group. Historically, the strong, aggressive, ruthless elements in a community have gained control of strategic advantages such as land, capital and other privileged positions from which they could dominate and exploit their fellows. This freedom of the dominant to exploit the subordinate is still the primary domestic relationship in every community based on private enterprise. In the same context, conquerors have enjoyed freedom at the expense of their defeated rivals and colonizers at the expense of native populations.

Freedom in the power age is in part the consequence of a cycle of development leading up to the efflorescence of freedom discussion, freedom theories and freedom practices in the West during the past two centuries, and their subsequent adoption by the peoples of Asia and Africa. This movement for political, economic and social freedom has been gaining in momentum and scope since the middle of the 18th century. It is based upon (1) the substitution of reason in place of tradition; (2) inquiry, discovery, invention, research; (3) more extensive utilization of nature and remodeling of society; (4) rising productivity, with the accompanying advances in production, wealth, education, leisure and opportunity for widening groups of people; and (5) with the consequent multiplication of quantity, variety and choices.

Human freedom in the power age is a consequence or derivative of four major factors:

1. Survival and continuity. If human life lasted for only one generation, it would consist, largely, of a struggle to exist. In effect it would be the kind of life that may be found in any jungle. An established culture pattern, preserved and enriched through generations, enlarges the possibilities of life and thus widens the margin of choices.

2. The second social factor in establishing and maintaining

26

freedom is a social equilibrium that is balanced and reasonably stable. Such a society functions effectively with a minimum of friction, tension and conflict. It is an axiom that the exercise of freedom depends upon a high degree of social stability and security.

3. Freedoms depend upon responsible performance of leaders and followers, well-organized and directed and accustomed to efficient team work. Specific freedoms depend upon responsible performance by groups of experienced persons doing their work on a basis of coordinated and disciplined division of labor. In the absence of such a foundation, freedoms would be few and far between.

4. The fourth social base for freedom is eternal watchfulness on the part of individuals, and coordinated group effort to maintain efficiency, keep burocracy to a minimum, exclude nepotism and other forms of favoritism, to eliminate corruption, to preserve widespread personal interest in the social apparatus and to maintain a high level of social consciousness and a keen sense of social responsibility.

Social balance, maintained with a minimum of friction and tension, responsible performance of leaders and followers in experienced well-administered teams accustomed to high levels of performance, plus eternal watchfulness and consciously co-ordinated group effort to equal or excel through economic and social planning should guarantee social survival, assure improvement and swing the course of community planning and practice away from restraint, toward larger individual and group freedoms.

Freedom is a consequence of group determination to master, control and direct the materials and forces of nature. Utilization of nature's resources depends in large measure upon the successful coordination and stabilization of social structure and social function. Freedom for humans is also bought by the forced labor of large numbers of "domesticated" or enslaved animals. Human freedom is not a derivative of nature but a consequence of individual and group activity. Its extension or restriction depends not primarily upon nature but upon the planned, coordinated actions of human beings.

## 6.   FREEDOM AS END OR MEANS

From the days of John Locke and John Milton to those of John Stuart Mill and the Mortimer Adler associates, many scholars and laymen have taken it for granted that freedom was an end in itself. One of the most recently published and most thoughtful books in the field, Herbert J. Muller's *Issues of Freedom*[18] contains a chapter titled "The Ends of Freedom" in which the author begins his presentation with the statement that the value of freedom might be called self-evident, a good in itself. Such thinking puts freedom in a class with objectives like the achievement of truth, harmony, beauty. The phrase "life, liberty and the pursuit of happiness" places freedom in the same category with survival and well-being.

Preservation of life may be considered as an end in itself, though it cannot stand alone in this regard, but is only one of an aggregate of human objectives. The same thing may be said of happiness and usefulness. They are parts of a considered patterned purpose. Aliveness and happiness are good in themselves, as are truth, harmony and beauty. To live and to be happy are states of personal being. Truth, harmony and beauty are states of universal being. One can live and be happy, but one cannot in the same complete sense be free. Life and happiness are complete in themselves. Freedom standing by itself is incomplete, a vacuum.

In order to complete the term "freedom" we must always qualify and circumscribe it. We must amplify by asking: free to do what? when? by what means? I may be free to drive up the street, but certainly I am not free to drive in a populated area at sixty miles an hour. Just as certainly I am never free to throw a rock through my neighbor's window except in an extreme emergency, to call or alert him. Nor am I free to break down his shrubbery, burn his garage or torture his children.

Freedom by itself is an incomplete term. Before it can be accepted and approved and acted upon it must be further described. If the direction which I take in the enjoyment of my freedom is considered a worthy one: to walk up the street—I am free. But if the direction is unworthy: to smash my neighbor's shrubbery, I am not free—morally or physically. If the neighbor sees me he will intervene and when the public authorities learn of my act, they will prevent it if they can. If they cannot prevent they will attempt to provide redress. If freedom of thought and choice leads to unworthy, immoral, dangerous or destructive actions, freedom disappears and is replaced by restraint.

Freedom is a means or device for achieving certain objectives. It is an instrument or agency which exists so long as it is used for worthy purposes. An unworthy use of freedom banishes freedom and opens the way to restraint. Freedom to be or to do may lead to consequences so varied and diverse that they may stand in sharp opposition one to the other. The determining factor is the objectives and purposes in the minds of those who are making and implementing their choices.

Like any tool, implement or agency, freedom is neutral. Most implements are designed for particular, specialized uses. An axe cuts; a hammer strikes; a file abrades; a shovel penetrates and separates masses of material. So long as these implements remain unused in the toolshed, they achieve none of their purposed objectives. To be effective they must be applied to particular tasks and aimed toward well-defined ends.

Axes, hammers and shovels, used productively, assist in building up. They may also be employed to tear down. A piece of metal shaped as a hoe may be used to till the soil and assist in the production of crops; shaped as a lethal weapon it may destroy property and take life. Of themselves implements are inert. Lying useless over a sufficient period of time they rust, decay and become useless. Purpose, energy and skill direct the use of implements and help to determine the consequences of their use.

Implements are not ends in themselves, but instruments or means. Ordinarily, they are used with objectives or ends in view. Temporarily they are enpurposed by the uses to which they are directed. When the purpose for which the implement is used has been achieved, the implement, having no purpose of its own, goes back into its place in the toolshed. Once again it is neutral or inert, and remains inert until it is again directed toward a purpose which the tool neither envisages nor shares.

Freedom is as neutral as any other means. The consequences of the exercise of freedom are determined by the causative and directive forces which are taking advantage of the possibilities which freedom presents.

Human propensities, proclivities, urges and purposes cover a wide range, from production and creation at one end of the scale to destruction and annihilation at the other. At certain times and under certain conditions the course of individual and group action moves in the direction of production and creation, with consequent expansion and fulfilment. At other times the reverse process sets in and the work of men's hands and the products of men's genius and the men themselves are demolished in nihilistic frenzy.

Freedom is permissive rather than purposive or intentional. It opens the way for feeling, thought, action. It offers a variety of choices and provides the possibility for decisions. Those who have freedom may make their decisions and determine their courses of action with an absence of restraint, compulsion, coercion. In this sense freedom is synonymous with opportunity. It opens the way, but is not the way, and does not determine the course or sequences of events.

Freedom, in the sense of opportunity, is neutral if not negative. It is not an object sought, nor does it point toward an object of desire. It merely opens the way to the achievement or fulfilment of the desire or purpose.

Freedom is a means rather than an end. Strictly speaking, it is not even a means in the sense that tools or weapons are means. Rather it is the absence of restraint or intervention, an opportunity for the free person to decide and function in the absence of compulsion or coercion.

*Part II*

# Freedom in Action

# 7. THE MULTIPLE DEMANDS FOR FREEDOM

One of the most impressive aspects of freedom in action is the multiple nature of the problem. Freedom is never unified or monolithic, except perhaps in its ideal or ideational aspect. Any examination of freedom in action reveals an overwhelming number and diversity of the fields in which freedom demands are being made. These demands fall into three broad groups: *first*, freedom of the individual in the relations which he experiences between his body, his emotions, his thinking, his imaginings, his aspirations; *second*, freedom for the individual in his relations with social groups; and *third*, freedom for social groups in their dealings with individuals and with each other.

FREEDOM OF MOVEMENT IN SPACE, or freedom to go and come arises primarily out of man's physical capacity to move about on the land. Technology has added movement on and under water, in the air and in space.

Historically, men have moved about a great deal: hunters pursuing game, herdsmen following pasture, migrants seeking new homes, conquerors intent on amassing wealth and power, merchants with their wares, travelers, students, scholars and persons bound on personal missions of one kind or another. Power age facilities have made movement so fast and comfortable that millions of travelers follow the seasons, and other millions (government officials and businessmen) go and come throughout the year.

Movement of peoples is accompanied by movement of goods, ideas and other products of man's ingenuity and labor. An interdependent world must exchange raw materials, capital goods, services, consumer supplies. It must also be prepared to have discoveries and inventions made in one part of the planet diffused rapidly to other places.

Uncontrolled movement of people, artifacts and ideas may lead to congestions, confusion, competition, tension, conflict. War, the most intensive form of conflict, has often been the spearhead of movement and a major factor in cultural diffusion. Both domestically and internationally, freedom of movement in space is urgently demanded, widely authorized, and frequently practised. It is limited, restricted or denied to chattel slaves, serfs bound to the land, to the subjects or victims of despotisms and to many subjects of power age sovereign states.

FREEDOM TO INQUIRE, INVESTIGATE AND KNOW is also basic. Man is as rational as he is curious. He observes, compares, contrasts, asks why. In present-day society he researches and experiments, makes and keeps records, draws conclusions and tries to express his theories in practice. The result is a growing body of knowledge. In some ages knowledge has been monopolized by priests, scholars, philosophers. Much of it is still "classified" and hidden. But the demand to know, plus the need for diffused knowledge in a complex culture, has led to the accumulation of knowledge in printed records stored in libraries and museums and accessible to inquirers.

At the core of curiosity, investigation and inquiry is man's desire to know the truth about himself and his surroundings. From the curiosity of children and backyard gossip to the passionate devotion of dedicated scientists or truth seekers, the desire to know is one of the controlling and dominating forces in human nature and in social life.

FREEDOM TO THINK AND UNDERSTAND is a logical product of the desire to know and of the accumulation and classification of knowledge. The inquirer wishes to follow where truth leads. To do that he must make assumptions, set up experiments, formulate deductions, verify his findings in the light of newly discovered information, and put theory into practice.

Men do not think in a vacuum. Their thought processes accumulate, arrange, digest and assimilate information as human food-tracts assemble, masticate, digest and assimilate food. Knowledge is the food for thought with which the scientists or engineers work. The demand for access to information and opportunity to put knowledge to work is one of the basic demands of artisans, engineers, scientists and philosophers.

FREEDOM OF BELIEF AND OUTLOOK is closely associated with the demand for freedom to discover, accumulate and use knowledge. Man knows some things; he has thought about some matters, but the range of his knowledge and his thought is small in comparison with the areas of the universe about which he knows little and has thought less. Through ages of experience men have learned to survive, to think ahead, to plan, to improve. The results of such achievements appear in the culture with which they surround themselves. But the sources of inspiration, intuition, revelation, the motive forces of light and life cannot be pinned down and dissected in a laboratory. They remain outside of and beyond the range of human experience and knowledge.

This is the area of speculation, belief, faith and hope. The same passion which men devote to the pursuit of knowledge leads them to speculate, to believe and develop theories, to formulate doctrines and organize authorities which propagate knowledge and faith. Consequent upon these developments are formulated religions, monopolies of rightness, arguments, contention, dissensions and wars in the name of promoting "the true faith".

Down through the ages faithists and scientists have collided. Faithists have clung to revelation, insight, intuition, tradition, authority. Scientists have pressed their inquiries and investigations,—penetrating, observing, describing and classifying, thus bringing segments of the unknown into the area of the known. The present age of research and discovery is characterized by coexistence and collaboration between established authority and the many individuals, private groups and public institutions which carry on the continued search for truth.

FREEDOM OF EXPRESSION covers the entire range of human exposition and communication. An experience may be customary, —the satisfying of hunger or the celebration of a festival. It may be intensely personal, as sex experience. It may be novel, a creative thought or act—a picture, a bit of carving, a revelation. Ordinarily it is more fully enjoyed when it is shared, at least in retrospect. Gregarious humans desire to share their customary and their new experiences with their fellows. There are a few introverts who live to themselves, but mankind as a whole burns with a desire for self-expression and a yearning to communicate feelings and thoughts to others. Among further aspects of communication are freedom to inform, suggest, advise,—as parents rear and guide children; formal presentation of experience orally and through the written word; teaching and preaching; employing the modern channels of communication, printing press, radio, television, camera; indoctrination, the science and art of propaganda; advertising.

Communication may take place through the arts: creative

writing, painting, sculpture, building, decoration, music, drama, dance. The arts offer a wide range of opportunity for man's expression, experiment and experience as creator, performer, teacher, or audience.

Sport,—physical prowess, competitive games, massed exhibitions, provide other avenues for the comparison and sharing of skills and for participation as well as audience amusement and diversion.

Crafts provide workmen and artists with an opportunity to display their skills and to share the output of their creative energies with those who use their products.

Professions enable those who will, to teach, heal, advise, guide, counsel, console and reassure their clients and followers.

Public associations are similarly widespread, covering the entire range of domestic and international affairs. This is the sphere of government, based upon consent, assent, inertia, ignorance, fear, awe, reverence, constitutions, bills of rights and resting finally upon the capacity of the governors to inform, enlighten, amuse, beguile, buy up, coerce, compel, imprison, and as a last resort, to take the lives of citizen-subjects.

Power age technology has resulted on one hand in coordination, on the other hand in bigness. Bigness has tempted the power-hungry to climb to the top and take control of the totalitarian apparatus. Bigness plus totalitarianism has dwarfed and downgraded the average individual to seeming helplessness and impotence unless he becomes part of a widespread network of organizations. In a very real sense the demand for association in the power age is a demand for the means of survival, expression and satisfaction of the life urge through group action. Surrounded by the towering organizational superstructure of power age society, the individual voices his demands and protects his interests most effectively by association with others in private and public groupings.

FREEDOM TO BE ALONE is a logical demand of those who spend their lives in unceasing contact with other humans. Man is social; at the same time he is an individual, conscious of his individuality, of his uniqueness and of his separateness from his fellows. Man's social nature demands association. Some of his individual urges demand separation and isolation. These dual and often contradictory aspects of human nature assert themselves and demand opportunity for expression. In the West, the demand for association has predominated. In the East, the demand for solitude holds an important place.

Seekers after solitude may desire to escape from the pressure of bigness, of centralized authority, of insistence upon conformity. They may wish to face themselves in quietude, to do creative work, to meditate, to contemplate nature. They may believe that they do all of these things better in solitude than in society, hence, for them the right to be alone, uninterrupted and undiverted, is essential.

POLITICAL FREEDOM FOR CITIZENS has been an urgent demand since the Middle Ages. Most of the literature on freedom and liberty, of the relation between the individual and the political state, deals with this issue. Some of it is devoted entirely to the distinction between subjects and citizens, and to a statement of civil or citizenship rights.

Demands for civil rights take many forms. *First* and most obvious is the determination and limitation of the role of government, the rights of citizenship, and a satisfactory balance between those who exercise authority and those over whom the authority is exercised. *Second* is initiative and referendum in selecting those public servants who exercise authority and in limiting their conduct in office and their term of office. *Third* is participation, directly or through representatives, in making public policy and carrying it into effect. *Fourth* is the formulation of procedure, in terms of unanimity, majority rule or some agreed relation among the citizenry. *Fifth* is the right of individuals and of minorities to dissent, to oppose and if need be to resist those in authority. This is the main theme of the 1776 Declaration of Independence. *Finally,* there is the demand that such rights should not only be recognized but should be written into covenants, constitutions, laws.

ECONOMIC FREEDOM has been the keystone of the arch upholding free enterprise and modern business. The demand came from a rising class of traders, fabricators and bankers hemmed in by restrictions imposed by landowners, hereditary aristocrats, military adventurers and more or less arbitrary rulers. Control of the means of production carries with it the possibility of shaping the course of private lives as well as public affairs.

Behind the conflict between landed aristocrats and businessmen there had been an age-old struggle for the best hunting grounds, the best pastures, the best farm land, and access to timber, minerals and other natural resources. Those who gained and held possession of nature's richest treasures lived more easily and with less expenditure of energy than their fellows. They even rented out the chance to work and lived on the proceeds without the need of producing their own livelihood.

Until recent times demands for economic freedom came chiefly from business enterprisers seeking wealth and power. It was not the hungry but the greedy who were striving to get rich. Recently the hungry and the dispossessed have been demanding economic freedom.

Demands for economic freedom have included the right to choose an occupation; to compete in the struggle for wealth; to acquire land and other forms of property; to tip the scales of equality (and even of justice) so that the greedy secured more than an even share of livelihood; to compete, first locally between individuals, then between rival local enterprises and finally between cities, nations and empires. The measure of success was the volume of wealth and power held by the victors in the survival struggle. The entire pattern of social organization was crystallized in property law which proclaimed the axiom: "To him that hath shall be given."

Latterly, associations of farmers and workers have presented new economic demands: the right to work and leisure, to a minimum wage and legally determined working conditions, to education and health, to social security. The Mexican Constitution of 1917 formulated these demands and wrote them into basic law. Today they appear in various constitutional provisions and statute laws,—particularly in the socialist countries.

Mid-twentieth century society is divided and rocked by the effort of rich, powerful nations to enjoy a more abundant livelihood than their poorer and weaker neighbors, and the demands of former colonial peoples for minimum standards of necessities, health, education.

FREEDOM TO DISCOVER, OCCUPY AND MAKE USE OF NATURE'S TREASURES has brought those making the demand into conflict with property, law and sovereignty. Man lives from the earth,— its vegetables and animals, its soil, forests, minerals, its power sources. On the principles of "first come, first served" and "possession is nine points in the law" each generation has laid claim to natural wealth and made the claim good while life lasted. Boundary lines were staked out and defended against outside "enemies." Usually when there was a struggle over property lines, the victor redrew the lines to include the property of his defeated rivals. The explosive expansion of Europe after 1450

42

resulted in a redividing and a redrawing of boundary lines on a planet-wide scale.

Beside the many demands for individual freedoms, demands for group freedom frequently parallel or dovetail with the demands of individuals. Groups, like individuals, demand freedom to make decisions and put them in practice. Group autonomy, initiative and sovereignty aim at the preservation, promotion and extension of group interests. Composite groups like villages, cities, states and nations are made of sub-groups or associations, each active in its own area.

On one hand there are private associations,—business, farm, professional, labor, educational, religious, social, sport. Next there are the legally constituted associations, which are licensed or charted by public authority: the family, the chartered non-profit and business corporations, and the chartered political groups,—municipalities, states and public corporations set up to perform specific functions. Third, there are established and recognized institutions or vested interests which have constitutions, franchises, charters, patents, copyrights, or which are supported by long established practice,—the state, the church, the military, education.

Each of these associations or legal entities presents demands for autonomy, independence, sovereignty, self-sufficiency. We have gone into some detail in listing individual freedom demands. Space prevents us from going beyond this brief classification of groups, each of which formulates its demands for freedom.

John Stuart Mill made two major efforts to discuss the subject of freedom. The first, *On Liberty*, emphasized freedom for the individual. The second, written shortly before his death, *On Social Freedom*, emphasized the multiple and social aspects of freedom. In the second work, Mill wrote, "People have commonly supposed that Freedom is one uniform thing, and that the free-

43

dom which one man may possess or desire is . . . the same sort of thing—differing only in degree—as the freedom which another man may possess or desire."[1] Not so, Mill continued, because "there are just a thousand million kinds of human freedom," including individual freedoms and group freedoms.

The numbers of freedoms in the power age have vastly increased. There has been an immense expansion in the variety of freedoms and the vast growth in the number and variety of individuals and groups demanding freedoms in the past half-dozen centuries that have marked the rise of western civilization. During the previous era, called variously the Middle Ages and the Dark Ages, the freedom idea was unacceptable and the action areas of freedom were narrow. The Renaissance and the Reformation re-introduced and broadened the idea of freedom. Modern man has spent much time and energy and suffered both victory and defeat in his efforts to formulate and implement his multitudinous freedom demands.

## 8. FREEDOM AND NECESSITY

Advocates who attempt to translate their freedom demands into individual or group action are face to face with two massive obstacles. The first is necessity. The second is conformity.

Necessity is defined under several headings: (1) the power of natural law that cannot be other than it is—natural causation—or physical compulsion imposed on man by nature; (2) anything that is inevitable, unavoidable; (3) the compulsion or constraint

44

of man-made circumstances such as custom, habit, law; (4) logical or moral considerations making certain actions inevitable or obligatory; (5) great or imperative need. In every one of the five categories, necessity limits or inhibits choice. Necessity does not ask or beg or implore; it demands, dictates, and will not be gainsaid.

In another volume we have described necessity as the web of circumstance, and have pointed out how arbitrarily human life in the present generation is circumscribed by natural and societal conditions over which modern man has little or no control.[2] To what extent does man's conscious participation in the development of an expanding universe circumscribe his freedom?

Freedom-necessity is a confrontation that has intrigued human beings at least during the period of written history. Words like "fate" and "destiny" and phrases like "the web of circumstance" are used to describe it. Thus far in discussing freedom in action we have written about man's choices, decisions and actions within the limits of nature as he finds it, within society as it exists and in man as he is. This web of current circumstance is the medium or milieu in which human life is carried on.

Men take part in making, repairing and destroying the web, particularly its societal aspects. They modify nature. They mature personally. Always the web of circumstance imposes its sharp and often harsh limitations on their lives.

Freedom, like other human concepts, is part of an equation or association with one or more of its opposites. Necessity is one of the chief opposites or opponents of freedom.

Necessity imposes limitations on freedom because necessity narrows both the range of choices and the extent to which they may be carried out in action. Under the pressure of necessity, restraint often enjoys priority, takes precedence over freedom, and frequently pushes the course of action to an extreme which virtually extinguishes freedom.

Most obvious among necessities are natural conditions and

forces. Human beings are born weak and almost helpless. At the other end of the life span they become senile and die. Birth and death are implacable necessities which sharply limit choices.

Human beings are land animals. If they wish to survive on water or in the air, they must make the necessary adaptations, such as boats or airplanes. When such devices fail to function, those who depend upon them suffer consequences, ranging from discomfort and inconvenience to death.

Other insistent necessities are air for the lungs, water and nourishment for the body's activity, relaxation, rest, sleep. The human organism is so constituted that failure to provide these essentials leads to serious consequences. There is a saying: "Three minutes without air, three days without water, and three months without food will end the earth-span of the average human." Extremes of heat, cold and pressure, over-exposure to the sun, high altitudes, great speeds may decrease human well-being to the vanishing point.

Certain materials are "poisonous" to human beings. Taken even in small quantities they cause discomfort, pain, death. Equally important is the chemical and physical balance which must be maintained in the human body if the organism is to function satisfactorily. The human organism is made up of water plus certain elements such as calcium, phosphorus, potash, sodium and a score of others. Some of these elements, like calcium in the bones, are abundantly present in the human body. Others such as iron, copper, iodine and boron exist in minute quantities. The relations of these chemical elements to one another are of such vital consequence that the over-abundance or lack of one or another of them may disturb, disrupt or terminate the normal functioning of the organism.

When body function is normal we describe the result as health. When it is abnormal we speak of disturbance, ill health or dis-

46

ease. Malfunction or disease is one of the generally experienced limitations on human freedom of action.

Change is another aspect of necessity. Human beings desire security if not certainty. Having won a status which provides conveniences, comforts and satisfactions arising from an established position, human beings seek to perpetuate these advantages, to share them among their relatives, friends and associates and to pass them on to their descendants. Such stability and security is challenged by one of the most inexorable aspects of necessity—the omnipresence of change.

Change may be thought of in space terms—change of place, or in status terms—change in social position. Change may be observed in the relations between associated units or in the processes and sequences which surround us and dominate every function of the human organism, of the social organism, of the cosmic organism. Attraction and repulsion, integration and disintegration, growth and decay, construction and destruction operate generally and continuously, disturbing and disrupting certainty, security and status.

Change follows patterns:—evolution, devolution, mutation, revolution. It also moves in cycles, such as the daily round or the sequence of the seasons. History likewise has cyclical features. Change also appears in accident, emergency, catastrophe. In every case it alters existing relations and associations.

Broadly speaking, change, as an aspect of necessity, disrupts and frustrates the best-laid plans of mice and men and limits their freedom to act in accordance with their choices.

Human beings are not bound completely by such necessities. They are able to modify or substitute up to a certain point. Beyond that point, however, they face hard and fast limitation. If they fail to conform to nature's requirements, they suffer or perish.

Two other categories of experience limit freedom; they may be grouped under emergencies and disasters. An emergency is an unexpected event which disturbs or upsets the accustomed course of existence. A disaster is an event which damages or destroys life and property over a large area. An emergency may overtake an individual or a community. Disaster usually designates large-scale disturbances which have serious consequences.

Emergencies range all the way from the birth of a baby, through accident, sickness, fire, flood, storm, drought, earthquake, to street fights, riots, revolts, rebellions, civil and international wars. Emergencies require departures from customary procedure. When they occur they disturb or upset the normal sequences of living and therefore demand immediate action designed to re-establish the normal conditions of life. During the emergency, freedoms are curtailed. The woman who is having a baby is not free to go on with her household routine. Fires, floods, droughts, earthquakes, tidal waves, riots and wars distract, obstruct and frequently prevent people from following their normal activities. Those who have been living uneventful lives are prevented by emergencies from following established routines. For better or worse, emergencies limit choices and coerce or compel individuals and social groups to alter habits and depart from customary courses of action.

Brief emergencies such as accidents may limit choices only temporarily. Floods which innundate large land areas or alter the course of rivers may lead not merely to the loss of individual property and life, but to general population displacement. Civil strife and international war may alter habitual and customary procedure for long periods of time, leaving the displaced victims who survive the emergency no choice but to begin life over again.

Emergencies and disasters are dealt with summarily and usually arbitrarily; the individuals involved being unable to make and carry out decisions. Communities are compelled to adopt measures designed to meet the emergency and mitigate the severity of the disaster. In sparsely settled areas and small communities, individuals, households and neighborhoods deal with emergencies and disasters as best they can. In larger population centers preparations are made in advance to meet emergencies if and when they arise. Equipment is available, materials are stockpiled, fire departments, health departments and departments of public safety are established and private associations are set up and equipped to take care of emergency situations.

One of the most universally employed techniques in every organized society is a declaration of emergency and the establishment of some type of martial law. Usually police or armed forces are called upon. Customary civil procedures are abrogated. In their places there is set up some type of arbitrary authority, exercising both the power to prevent and prohibit and the power to conscript and compel. Under such circumstances freedom is reduced and restraint is increased to a point which, in the judgment of those in authority, is required to meet the emergency or deal with the disaster.

Power age society presents the juxtaposition of freedom in action and of restraint in action. Both freedom and restraint are present in every organized community. Under favorable conditions, the area of freedom is enlarged and stabilized. When necessity demands, freedom is restricted or abrogated in favor of restraint.

There are necessities imposed by nature, arising out of association and connected with personal life which narrow choices often to the vanishing point. When those necessities arise, they demand priority and get it. They may be fleeting or of relatively long duration. They may be local or of wider scope, but when necessity demands, freedom is reduced or extinguished.

49

There is another aspect of necessity and freedom which cannot be ignored. Necessity not only limits freedom; it also demands and compels actions looking toward freedom. It is necessary, at a certain point, to separate or free a baby from the body of its mother. If the liberation fails to take place, both mother and child suffer dire consequences. Necessity compels the newborn child to breathe, to move, to cry out. As the child matures, it is under the necessity of expressing itself physically, emotionally, mentally, socially. In each of these instances necessity compels the individual to make choices and follow consequent courses of action. Here is a contradiction or duality which might be described as compulsory freedom.

Maturing individuals, at various stages of their lives, feel an inner urge to express themselves—physically, emotionally, intellectually, socially, cosmically. The consequence of such urges are creative thoughts and acts in the crafts, arts and sciences, in social relations. The creative artist, the inventor, the social reformer, the teacher, the prophet are under great pressure to accept the current patterns of conduct and follow customary procedures. Normally they yield to such pressures, and suffer the depression and frustration that accompany defeat. In many cases, however, they defy restraint, express their emotions and ideas, and take the consequences.

Similarly, freedom often becomes a necessity in the lives of groups as they mature. Differences appear between sections and factions; disagreement leads to factionalism, and eventually the group splits into two or more segments. All social groups pass through divisive, schismatic, fragmentive experiences.

Freedom and necessity present a basic juxtaposition in the lives of individuals and communities. Necessity is demanding and compelling for groups as for individuals, whether the results limit freedom or enlarge it. Men yearn for freedom but yield to necessity, which encircles, contains and limits freedom by restricting the area or areas of choice, decision and action.

## 9. FREEDOM AND CONFORMITY

Necessity does not stand alone as a general restrictive on freedom in action. Conformity also limits freedom. Necessity, particularly in its emergency aspects, operates only occasionally and sporadically. Conformity is a constant, insistent, insidious force which not only pushes the individual and the social group into a strait-jacket but smothers their heads in blankets.

Much of necessity derives from nature. Conformity involves acceptance of social pressures and obedience to social behests. Necessity commands. Conformity wheedles, coaxes, cajoles and threatens. Most human beings, most of the time, bow before necessity. Indeed, they have no alternative. Whether they like it or not, they must make their choices and shape their lives within the limits which necessity imposes. In a slightly different context, they are the prisoners of conformity.

Conformity is thought or action in harmony with some standard, pattern or principle, hence the phrase "conform to specifications." In its derivation, conformity means to take or abide by form. The term is a broad one, used in technology, in the arts, in law, in philosophy, in psychology, in social relations and practices. Adaptation is a more or less voluntary adjustment to new or different conditions. Conformity means action in harmony with an established and insistent social standard or pattern.

Conformity begins at birth, when new arrivals start learning how things are done by other human beings. Up to a certain point, conformity is voluntary. Infants imitate or mimic their associates, whether they be youngsters or adults. Imitation in gestures, in speech, in action, is part of the adaptation to a new environment. In families with several children, it is the youngsters who take the newcomer in hand and show him how to behave.

The newcomer enjoys imitating. Uncertainty and insecurity lead him to take social roots and belong to a social group. As the newcomer grows in dexterity and proficiency he joins in group activities,—in games, sports, rituals. In all his moves he is shown, directed, guided. Group activities have their patterns. Newcomers are invited to join in the game, are taught the rules, and admonished to abide by them. If they fail to conform, either through ineptitude or design, they are reprimanded: "Don't spoil the game. This is the way we always do it." At a later stage: "Who are you to make your own rules or to stay out of the game? Come on. Get in. Do it our way." If leadership appears and is recognized by the group, conformity is again demanded and obedience is enforced. "Hey you, line up and do as the others are doing."

While this pressure toward conformity is preparing the newcomer to adapt to established customary procedures, parents, teachers and other adults are doing their part to guide, train and direct the course of development on the theory that as the twig is bent, so will the tree incline.

Gardner Murphy, in a chapter on The Internationalization of Social Control, notes three parallel child reactions to conformity requirements. First there is the demand to be admitted, based upon a desire for love, attention and a place in the group. Then comes protest against exclusion on the grounds of immaturity.

52

Third, there is individual rebellion against interference with primitive impulses and having to subordinate self-expression to group demands.[3]

Social pressure to conform, which begins in the home at birth, continues in childhood, youth and throughout adult life. Conformity promotes convenience and increases the comfort of all concerned. In any type of teamwork, it improves efficiency, smooths out difficulties and increases the chances of success in carrying out group projects. Consequently it is rewarded with recognition, approval, promotion, responsibility and participation in leadership.

Conformity is not merely a stabilizing force in any type of group activity. It is one of the essential elements in group survival and in attaining group objectives. In every group, from the family through various voluntary associations to such public institutions as the school, the village, the city and the state, the acceptance of tradition and participation in customary practices are looked upon as among primary social virtues.

Louis Hartz wrote[4] that at the bottom of the American experience of freedom, not in antagonism to it but as a constant element in it, there has always been the assumption of conformity. Hartz quotes Santayana as stating that what is best in America is compulsory. One might go further and report that most communities consider it proper and advisable to wait for the initiative and follow the lead of the "best" people.

Developing, improving and disseminating culture traits and building them into the daily round of ideas, outlooks and practices of individuals and social groups is a major preoccupation of human beings. Social groups depend for their continued existence and their growth upon success in promoting acceptance and conformity.

John Stuart Mill in his essay *On Social Freedom*[5] justified restrictions on individual freedom and conformity to established social patterns by recognizing that there are "limits beyond which we cannot hope to extend our freedom without doing away with those conditions which render life valuable to us." Stated in these terms, a life pattern is a compromise between freedom demands and conformity requirements, in which freedom ends where conformity begins.

Another factor, even more restrictive, is the relation between freedom and social continuity. Freedom presupposes choices, decisions and actions here and now. Conformity insists that the rising generation accept institutions and practices inaugurated or adopted and followed by previous generations. Conformity shackles choice, decision and action, thus enabling the dead hand of the past to throttle the present and shape the future.

Freedom and conformity in action have been tested out repeatedly in recent times in a laboratory provided by United States and other frontier areas. Results of these tests have been consistently uniform in at least one respect—conformity has broadened its grip on the community while freedom has been restricted or diminished.

On the American frontier life was free and easy. Land was free (after it had been taken from the native populations by brute force). Competition was fierce and raw. Gambling and brigandage were legitimate sources of livelihood. Individual courage, quickness and resourcefulness were prime survival qualities. Risk often paid off handsomely. Somewhere, in a far-off city, there was a shadowy institution called Government. On the frontier, grab-and-keep was the rule of the road. Such situations were almost as free politically and socially as they were economically. Life was fluid. Men made their decisions and embodied them speedily in action, without let or hindrance.

Frontier life continued in some of the western states until the last years of the 19th century. It persisted into 20th century Alaska. It still lives in western stories, poems, plays, movies, where the natives, a lesser breed, are driven from their hunting grounds; the hero struggles manfully, surmounts obstacles, survives and prospers, while the villain is defeated, humiliated, liquidated.

Take a trip through these former frontier areas. They are still crass and crude in spots, but they tend to look like every other part of the United States. Paint and chrome finish have replaced shabbiness and neglect; shacks have yielded to rows of suburban villas. Law and order are painfully in evidence. Freedom, in both speech and action, is sharply restricted. Young and old in the rapidly growing cities that have replaced many frontier towns toe the mark, and conform to the pattern of the American Way of Life more completely than their fellow citizens in older communities.

Experience seems to prove that the joys of freedom are less attractive to settled human communities than the comforts and satisfactions which accompany conformity. Freedom predominated for entire generations on the frontier. In every case it was down-graded in favor of widespread and thorough-going conformity. As frontier communities grew in size and complexity, the need for law and order increased and the premium on conformity rose.

Conformity is the synthesis and consequence of social pressures designed to persuade or, if necessary, to compel individuals and sub-groups to adopt the folkways, learn the rules and stay in line with the outlooks and practices of the dominant elements of the community.

Propagandists for the status quo advocate freedom and at the same time preach the American Way of Life, which is not free. If people in the United States or any other country were free, individuals would choose their way of life for themselves and choose it as they live along from day to day and year to year. They would also change their life patterns as often as they saw fit. There would be countless ways of living in one neighborhood or community, as well as in countries and continents.

The American Way is a conformist way, a modification of the British Way, the French Way, the Dutch Way, with roots far back in a European background of long-past generations. If young America accepts and follows the American Way it is not following the path to freedom but is conforming to tradition and custom.

## 10.  *THE PROMISE OF FREEDOM*

Peoples in search of better living conditions have multiplied their demands for freedom during recent years. Dissatisfied with the limitations, restraints and oppressions of the established social order and increasingly aware of the possibilities and opportunities inherent in a rational way of life, they were ready to make a change. Freedom offered an alternative to restraint and coercion. They took the offer and chose freedom, assuming that when they were free their problems would be resolved and they would be secure, comfortable, happy.

Freedom was accepted as an end in itself, as axiomatic as "life" and "happiness." Hence the oft-repeated phrase "life, liberty and the pursuit of happiness." Freedom was regarded as one of the most treasured possessions of mankind. Indeed, among the freedom advocates, there were many who insisted that in a listing of the desirable objectives of human life, freedom came first.

This attitude has been particularly prominent in the self-designated "free world." The philosopher Horace Kallen lists the outstanding features of modern culture as "science, democracy, machine industry, peace. Each has its own individuality. . . . All, nevertheless, are sprung from a common impulsion and own a common drive. This impulsion, this drive, is freedom."[6] Gilbert Cannon wrote: "The grand problem of society is the establishment of freedom for the greatest possible number."[7] The history of the world, according to Hegel, "is nothing but the development of the idea of Freedom."[8] "Since Spirit is self-contained existence, the essence of Spirit is Freedom."[9] Hamilton believes that freedom stands, "more than any other word, for the possibilities of human attainment. . . . In the conscious striving after social improvement, freedom is and must remain the holy grail."[10] "Europe stands and falls with freedom."[11] "Only respect for freedom can give final beauty to men's lives," writes Laski.[12] Again and again leaders of modern thought have extolled freedom and sought release from restraints, restrictions, compulsion, coercion. Present-day political discussions are studded with references to the doctrine that freedom comes first.

Despite apostrophes to freedom uttered by western spokesmen, feudal property and class relations persisted in Central Europe until 1945. They have been continued in Spain down to the present day. Paralleling this survival of feudal restraints and restrictions in the freedom-professing West, between 1500 and 1900, all of the Americas, Africa and Australia and much of Asia were conquered, occupied, ruled and exploited by West Europeans. They took possession in the names of their respective sovereigns, settled down, built themselves homes on the best land, appropriated the resources, hired or conscripted local labor power, set up governments and enriched themselves at the expense of the native populations, all in the name of freedom. To this pattern of conquest, subjugation and exploitation western civilizers added the African slave trade and established extensive slave economies in the Americas. The structure of world society during the modern period of western civilization was a classical example of compulsion and coercion imposed by white European masters upon colored native populations.

Internationally, western civilization had established a pattern of imperial coercion and compulsion to which freedom demands were the logical answer. Domestically a parallel situation existed. Some of the builders of 19th century European empires preserved serfdom until the middle of the present century. They preserve hereditary monarchies and aristocracies and have maintained state-supported religious organizations down to the present day. All of them maintain a system of private property in land and other means of production and a wage system under which labor power is bought and sold in the open market. All of them permit and encourage the rich and powerful to enrich and empower themselves at the expense of the poor and virtually defenseless masses.

Against this pattern of chattel slavery, serfdom, colonial servitude, despotism, profiteering and exploitation, agitators and reformers raised their voices and presented their programs in the name of freedom. So widespread was this demand and so popular with the masses of mankind that in the present century even leaders of conservative parties have used the "freedom" slogan as an effective means of engaging the attention of inert, indifferent and despondent victims of tyranny, repression and exploitation. Thus President Woodrow Wilson wrote of "the new

58

freedom," President F. D. Roosevelt of "the four freedoms," and Presidents Truman and Eisenhower of "the free world."

Advocates of the freedom cult have attempted to further both individual and group interests in the name of freedom. Their demands for economic freedom, or *laissez faire,* when put into action were used to advance the fortunes of a developing business class hampered by feudal restrictions. Similar arguments were advanced to justify, not merely the expansion of the economy, but the extension of political frontiers and the alteration of the social structure. The world-girdling 19th century empires were built as expressions of freedom to trade, freedom to exploit and freedom to annex and occupy essential or strategic territory. In the same freedom context, national boundaries were altered and culture patterns were modified.

Such expansionist and imperialistic policies were carried out by aristocracies, monarchies and oligarchies which pursued their own class interests without consulting their home populations. As capitalism and imperialism matured during the 18th and 19th centuries, workers in the imperial homelands organized and resisted. Protests came increasingly from the middle classes and the intelligentsia as colonial peoples sabotaged, boycotted and re-volted. Parliamentary debates in Britain at the time of the American Revolution showed strong opposition to existing imperial relations. The rise of socialism during the 19th century was an expression of the public opposition to imperialism and to the wars which imperialism entailed.

Carried to its logical outcome in 19th century imperialism-colonialism, freedom to expand capitalist economies and to occupy foreign-inhabited territory led to two inescapable consequences. One was a series of trade wars, arms races, local wars and finally the great war of imperial rivalry and survival which began early in the present century and has continued intermittently down to the present day. The other consequence was colonial unrest, resistance and rebellion.

Such policies, carried out frequently in the name of freedom, have led to tyranny and despotism which were detrimental to individuals and strong minority groups in the imperial centers as well as in the colonies. They also resulted in the impoverishment, bankruptcy and even in the destruction of the nations and empires involved in the survival conflicts.

Peoples who have been attracted by the promises of freedom and frequently have offered their lives in struggle for freedom's assumed benefits, may be grouped under nine headings.

CHATTEL SLAVES, whether shanghaied, sold, or born into a condition which gave their owners and masters the right to compel obedience on pain of jail, torture and death, looked upon emancipation from bondage as the first step toward a good life.

SERFS OR PEONS, attached to the land and bought and sold with the land like any other chattel were only one step removed from slavery. Like slaves they believed that liberation from serfdom would end their troubles and open up attractive vistas of ease, comfort and happiness.

SMALL ENTERPRISERS, including farmers, who owned at least a part of their means of livelihood, demanded freedom from bigness on one hand and monopoly on the other. These "little people" often depended on marginal activities which could meet the consequences of bigness and monopoly only by becoming big in their turn or by long hours of labor under exacting working conditions. In practice, freedom has not solved their problem because, in a very real sense, it was free enterprise which gave them their chance to compete and then eliminated most of them in the competitive race for wealth and power and drove many of them from the level of independent enterprisers into the ranks of the exploited wage earners.

LANDLESS LAND WORKERS AND JOBLESS JOB SEEKERS are both in the same leaky boat. Both seek to make a living in a social pattern which justifies and legalizes land ownership and job ownership by one individual or group, and the leasing out of these opportunities to work for a living under conditions profitable to the owners. In the power age, with sharp limitations upon the amount of available land and the large-scale units of economic enterprise, the demand for free land or free jobs has no meaning. Escape from the insecurity and uncertainty which job-seeking entails lies in cooperative or group ownership of the jobs upon which members of the cooperating group depend for their livelihood. It is a reorganization of the social pattern, and not freedom, which will bring relief to those who suffer from underemployment.

VICTIMS OF CASTE, CLASS AND COLOR DISCRIMINATION, SEGREGATION AND EXPLOITATION cannot hope for freedom so long as these restrictive patterns remain in existence. As individuals they may gain relief through success in the competitive struggle, but the process of liberation must continue until the causes which give rise to discrimination and segregation have been removed.

VICTIMS OF POLITICAL TYRANNY have demanded and sought freedom from the earliest periods of written history. For them freedom from tyranny offers relief, unless the new leader becomes a tyrant in his turn, in which case the victim moves from one tyranny to another and is never really freed. This situation presents a real dilemma which can be solved only when humanity has discovered and applied adequate safeguards against tyranny and despotism.

COLONIAL PEOPLES conquered, occupied and exploited by foreigners may win freedom from foreign domination, but if their real problem is landlessness, joblessness, or inferiority due to marginal land or economic and social backwardness, independence from foreign domination will merely transfer control over their lives from a foreign master to a domestic one. During the past two centuries many colonial peoples in the Americas, Asia and Africa have won independence from foreign domination only to find that their real problems do not lie in freedom but in a drastic reorganization of the social pattern which perpetuates their dependency and servility.

EXPLOITED, WAR-RIDDEN PEOPLES in the centers of imperial power are particularly vehement in their demands for freedom. Some of them have gained the comforts, securities, diversions and opiates which job-owning minorities of industrially developed countries are able and willing to provide for those who live in welfare states. But such peoples have neither secured nor enjoyed freedoms. They have merely exchanged their collars of wood, rope and leather for silver and gold-plated collars of iron or some lighter alloy. Those who willingly or unwillingly continue to wear their collars are provided with propaganda blinders which keep their eyes on the opportune chance and button their lips, lest they speak out of turn. As power age society evolves and the capitalist social pattern becomes less workable and more obsolete, freedom becomes a more and more empty name for job-slavery, brain-washing and enforced conformity to a pattern which obviously advances the interests of the rich and powerful job-owners at the expense of the poor and powerless job-takers.

FREEDOM DEMANDS COME FREQUENTLY FROM IDEALISTS outraged by needless suffering, injustice and inefficiency and the slowness of social change, who are eager to move rapidly into a social pattern that will bring men nearer to realizing their loftiest aspirations and satisfying their hearts' most exalted desires. In a very real sense idealists and meliorists are the eyes, ears, hearts, minds and consciences of each community. Some citizens are so busy looking after their own affairs that they have neither time

62

nor thought for the general welfare. Others are amusing themselves. Still others are preoccupied with the trivial details of life. Many never give a thought to public business. Idealists and meliorists often neglect their own affairs because with them matters which concern the general public have first place in their thoughts and actions. Their demands for freedom are entitled to early and serious consideration because they put the general welfare at the top of their priority listings.

This inventory of the major groups that have been lured by the promises of freedom will not satisfy the more ardent freedom devotees. In some obvious cases such as chattel slavery and peonage, the first step toward a better life for victims of such practices *must* be liberation. In other cases such as small enterprisers trying to make a living on their own in the complex power age world, freedom is meaningless jargon. Victims of racial, caste and class discrimination will not get relief through demands for freedom. What they need is a change in social relations and institutions.

Freedom, like other concepts, is fruitful for human beings in particular situations. The mere repetition of the "freedom! freedom!" slogan is as idle, bootless and disillusioning as any other unfulfilled or unfulfillable promise. Any unbalance or maladjustment, whether individual or social, should be examined on its merits. When all of the evidence is at hand, the case should be diagnosed and relief should be provided. A general prescription of "freedom" as an answer for all individuals and all social situations is unsatisfactory and, under certain conditions, it may be as dangerous as any other guaranteed universal cure-all.

## 11.  *THE MENACE OF FREEDOM*

As one intense emotion, such as love or hate, is easily transmuted into its opposite, freedom as promise may be transformed readily into freedom as menace. In view of such a possibility, freedom advocates must present a bill of particulars when they prescribe freedom as an answer to the problems confronting individuals and social groups. What do they mean when they talk generally about freedom? Freedom for whom? To do what? When? Where? How? Until these questions are answered, increased doses of freedom may worsen adverse conditions which they were supposed to remedy.

In the previous chapter we pointed out that freedom promises were not effective unless they met particular situations and dealt with specific difficulties at the right time. Freedom as a blessing today might, under new conditions, become a danger and a curse tomorrow.

Crimes endanger the general welfare of a community. Freedom for criminals would be a menace to community interests. The community therefore forbids crime, adopts a criminal code listing a great variety of acts which are considered prejudicial to community well-being, and prescribes penalties for lawbreakers. Individuals and social groups who violate the criminal law are restrained and coerced. The nature of crime depends upon local custom or accepted practice. In this very considerable area, by common consent, freedom is officially abrogated, and restraint and coercions are relied upon to protect the community.

Examples of the menace of freedom may be picked up at random outside of the area covered by the criminal code. Freedom ceases to be a promise and becomes a menace when its exercise leads to the subjugation of one human being to the will of others, of one group to the will of other groups or when its exercise undermines the general welfare. One of the most obvious examples of the transmutation of freedom from promise to menace is provided by the adoption of laissez faire and the rise of free enterprise.

Free enterprise advocates of the Adam Smith period[13] contended that freedom to acquire and accumulate private property and employ it in the open market in a competitive effort to acquire additional wealth would result in reasonable profits, just prices and fair wages, and would, as a matter of logic, justify the continued use of competition as the soundest means of maintaining a balance between the various types of economic activity, the various claimants to income and the stability, security and progress of the whole society. The one requirement was that government keep its hands off the economic process and allow the contending forces in a free market to work out economic relationships in accordance with "natural law." Laissez-faire, applied to various fields of free enterprise, has failed to produce the peace, prosperity and freedom which its advocates anticipated. On the contrary, during the first half of the present century, after having a free field for its development during the hundred years that followed the Napoleonic Wars, western society organized in terms of free enterprise has been torn and shattered by war, depression, rebellions and revolutions. In the mid-20th century laissez-faire has ceased to be a promise and has become a menace to human well-being.

Consequences so divergent from anticipations are not accidental or coincidental. They arise from the exercise of those freedoms upon which the champions of laissez-faire based their hopes for a peaceful, prosperous, happy future.

Freedom to own land or other property in any amount (private ownership of the means of general livelihood) enabled the shrewd, well-equipped, unscrupulous rich to become richer. To stabilize their position, they organized and increased their control over the state. Through their control of state power they were able to secure laws, patents, charters and franchises that still further increased their wealth and power. They were then in a position to introduce a new principle into the market: the law of monopoly prices. Instead of increased production, competition and lowered prices, monopolists produced the minimum volume that would yield the maximum profit. Under this principle the monopolists were able at the same time to increase both prices and profits. Freedom for economic monopolists raised prices and imposed hardship on the consuming public.

A new factor entered the market—workers also organized. At the outset such moves were labeled "conspiracy" by the free enterprisers and punished under laws enacted by governments dominated by the job-owning exploiters. Eventually two powerful organizations faced each other. Job-owners and job-takers battled relentlessly in the economic or class war and fought to determine the proportion of income going for profits on one hand and wages on the other.

Thus free enterprise under its own rules in its own "free" market was pushed from the center of the stage by monopoly, partial or total. Under the new conditions, the market which had been free only in theory, was "rigged," "fixed" and manipulated by the monopolists until they had converted competitive enterprise into monopoly capitalism and destroyed the free market which competitive enterprise was designed to promote.

Freedom to exploit passed through a similar metamorphosis.

66

Under the principles of laissez-faire, job-owners competing for labor power with other job-owners fixed a "reasonable" wage for job-takers. In fact, however, the workers even when organized were always at a disadvantage. Job-takers were poor and had to eat. Job-owners, rich and under no immediate pressure to produce, could afford to wait. With starvation on the side of the job-owners, the result was usually predetermined. The principle of exploitation—"you work, I eat" was established in practice, recognized in law and institutionalized in "securities" or titles to ownership which enabled the holder to collect interest and dividends. The owner need do no work in order to live; the one requirement was ownership. Thus the pattern of unearned income became one of the pillars of the bourgeois world. In the course of the class struggle between job-owners and job-takers, under free enterprise rules, the large assured incomes went to the job-owners because they owned the property. Instead of even-handed justice in the economy, one group worked for a living while the other group lived by owning. Per family worker incomes were small. Per family owners' incomes were large, under a system which gave priority not to the producer but to the parasite, living on unearned income. Freedom to exploit and pay job-owners unearned income divided communities into warring classes. It also institutionalized injustice, favoring the parasites and penalizing the workers.

Freedom to waste undermines the general welfare in free enterprise society. There are many aspects of waste—waste of natural resources such as forests, top soil and water (all in part replaceable); and waste of metals and minerals found in the earth's crust (which when used up are gone for good); waste in the production of non-essential or shoddy goods and services; waste of unused productive capacity; waste of human health, energy, hopes, aspirations; and last but not least, especially in a power age, the waste of war. We need not give details under these headings. It is only necessary to read the press, listen to the radio, watch television, and travel here and there in "the richest nation in the world," which at the same time is the most wasteful nation on earth.

Freedom to waste began in North America's colonial days, when resources were deemed "inexhaustable." Men burned trees to get rid of them, shot to near-extinction bison and pigeons for the joy of killing, used the land until it was exhausted, abandoned it to water and wind erosion, and moved onto new free land. If Professor Paul Sears, in *Deserts on the March,* is right in assuming that civilized man has converted fertile land masses into deserts by deforestation, over-grazing and open cultivation, and that modern man has carried the process faster and further than his predecessors, then waste of natural resources under free enterprise is robbing mankind of the foundation upon which life and well-being depend. If Professor A. J. Toynbee, in *A Study of History*, is justified when he asserts that all the civilizations known to history have been destroyed in the first instance by war, the present generation, following a policy of the free, planless conversion of irreplaceable natural resources into quick profits for the monopolist and arming free competing sovereign nations with mass destructive agencies, is busy digging the grave of yet another civilization. Again freedom to exploit and compete has been converted from a promise into a menace on a scale so vast that it threatens the well-being and survival of the entire human race.

Freedom to corrupt provides another example of the menace which may lie in the exercise of freedom. Freedom to lie, to bribe, to drug, to dissipate, to prostitute are part of the freedom to corrupt. We begin with lying because in business as in public relations, the power age has raised lying to the level of a science and

68

an art. The most obvious form of business lying is advertising. The most shameful is the profession of one moral code and the practice of another. Such duplicity and hypocrisy also extend to the professions,—first and most outstanding, to diplomacy; second, law, then teaching, and finally preaching. A lie is the deliberate misrepresentation of known facts. The professions to-day practice misrepresentation deliberately, in order to increase the wealth and enhance the power of their pay-masters.

Space does not allow of detail. Bribery, drugging, prostitution and dissipation are under-cutting the physical stamina, the mental balance and the moral sense of the American and other Western people as they have degraded the human beings who built previous civilizations. Schemers learned a long time ago that it is more profitable to pander to human vices than to augment human virtues. Hence the pandemonium of appeals which free enterprisers and free-booters direct against the public through the many channels of information and propaganda which science and technology has placed at the disposal of the corrupters. Freedom to corrupt begins by demoralizing the corrupters. It eventuates in honey-combing the social structure.

Two things are certain. First, until the present game is played out, private enterprisers and free-booters will continue to make profit at the expense of a public which is gullible and usually is at least one step behind their would-be corrupters. While shrewd, greedy and unscrupulous men are free to corrupt, they will continue to pull down an over-mature society faster than the builders are able to restore it.

Another freedom which has been exercised persistently in the political field is freedom to take over the apparatus of government. At times, power seizure involves the use of armed force. At other times, power is taken by guile, in the name of freedom, and is paid for with bread and circuses. Power seizure by whatever means undermines security, threatens war and wastes the hard-won gains of the builders. Freedom to take power is one of the basic rights asserted in the Declaration of Independence. Time out of mind this freedom has been exercised. With few exceptions it has led into despotism.

How easy it is to assert, in each instance where authority is challenged, that freedom will be advanced by a seizure of power. The recent history of independence movements has been littered with the tyrannies and despotisms established in the name of freedom. Not alone in Latin America, the classical home of the modern coup d'etat, has authority been upset by freedom fighters, among whose camp followers were the future tyrants and despots, with the manacles ready-fashioned to snap around the wrists and ankles of the unwary. Once the apple-cart of community life is upset, the chances are ten to one that the scattered fruit will be grabbed by the shrewd, the greedy and the unscrupulous. If this is true in the next instance as it has been true a thousand times in the past, the promises of freedom through power seizures will be swallowed up by the menace of tyranny and despotism.

Power to destroy threatens every community with disruption. Usually the destroyers are secretive, competent, experienced and strategically placed. Almost always they appear in sheep's clothing as patriots, guardians of honor, defenders of home and fireside, promoters of this and that freedom. Whatever rationalization they employ, they remain professional destroyers.

Builders and destroyers are at work in every community as they are in every cell and organ of every human body. So long as the builders keep ahead of the destroyers, the organism, biological or social, grows and develops. When the builders hesitate or falter, the destroyers, only a few steps behind, overtake and pass the builders, whereupon the biological or social structure begins to decay and disintegrate.

Military forces are trained to destroy. To be sure, they are pledged to spread havoc abroad rather than at home. Let them win the mastery, however, often in the name of freedom, and seizure of power and civil war will follow unless the destroyers are dislodged from their power positions. If the warriors are defeated, the enemy does the destroying and plundering in the defeated homeland. If the destroyers win in the military struggle, after reducing the enemy to rubble, all too frequently they return to the homeland, divide into factions and fight over the spoils which victory has brought.

Wars are fought occasionally. Between military struggles, the apparatus of the destroyers bankrupts the treasury in the name of defending freedom, endangers the economy by making it rest on the easy money that comes from military contracts, and corrupts public morality by teaching that the end justifies the means and that armed might makes right.

History and current experience with freedom granted to the wrong people, at the wrong time, in the wrong cause, turns freedom from promise into menace and produces the opposite of its declared purpose. It is not enough to make free. Before individuals or communities get the green light on freedom proposals they must answer the questions: freedom for whom; to do what, where, when and by what means?

Misadventures with freedom have led even former freedom fighters to turn their backs and fly from freedom into the arms of restraint, compulsion and coercion. The masses of mankind suspect freedom as a result of many bitter experiences or else they turn away from the struggle for freedom to gorge themselves on comfort, amusement, diversion and other soporifics.

Eric Fromm has written a book, *Escape from Freedom,* in

which he discusses the entire subject, primarily from a psychological point of view.[14] The Renaissance, he notes, enabled certain groups to escape from the feudal pattern, but it left the individual alone, fearful, bewildered, in a new and unknown social environment. People cannot endure this solitude. The avenue of escape is submission to a leader or a pattern of compulsive social conformity. Fromm crystallizes his argument in a question: what does freedom mean to modern man and why and how does he try to escape from it? As we have noted, in recent decades, while freedom demands have multiplied and freedom struggles have increased, not only have disruption and destruction been widespread but the period has been marked by a general retreat from freedom and the return to authoritarian and totalitarian social patterns.

After centuries of experimentation with various types of freedom, the last five decades have been marked by broadening military preparations, carefully planned widespread physical destruction, resulting in instability, insecurity, anxiety, fear and organized hatred, and by the fear of freedom and the flight from freedom. In the consequent stampede away from freedom and its menaces, oligarchies have imposed multiple restrictions including military conscription, forced labor, government by executive order, the police state, physical torture and other forms of terror. If the 18th and 19th centuries were swayed by the promises of freedom, the 20th century may well recoil and retreat before the menaces of freedom.

strictions, and subordinate economic and social relations to the diplomatic and military manoeuvers requisite for carrying on the cold war against marxism and communism.

"Free world" powers support private enterprise and representative government based on popular elections. They emphasize the individual, his rights and dignity, a competitive struggle for material success and for advancement in the status hierarchy. Beside the major western powers the "free world" includes countries with little free enterprise and less representative government, which accept "free world" policy decisions, provide raw materials, investment opportunities and markets for manufactures, receive economic aid from the major "free world" nations, and frequently are occupied by "free world" military forces and installations.

The "free world" is the child of the Renaissance, the Reformation, the industrial revolution, the rise of laissez-faire economy and of representative, republican government. Revival of East-West trade a thousand years ago, at the time of the Crusades, helped to start a movement toward the build-up of modern western nations. This movement reached its zenith in the planet-girdling empires organized between 1500 and 1900. Feudalism waned during this period. Capitalism, aided by the development of science and technology, moved to the center of the world stage. Until the middle of the 18th century, freedom was thought of as the easing of feudal restrictions, an opportunity for business and professional men to advance their interests, and for the new states that were winning their independence to defend and promote their sovereign rights. In most cases the sharp lines separating titled or landed gentry from commoners, who busied themselves with merchandising, construction, manufacturing and banking, grew fainter or were eliminated as landlords invested in business enterprise and businessmen bought landed estates and married their children into families of the

tions of political importance and even of political power, the picture changed sharply. Not only has the power pattern been drastically altered, down-grading West and Central Europe and pushing non-European nations into top positions, but the "free world" has, perforce, abandoned its century-long pattern of aggression and gone on the defensive. The central problem for "free world" statesmanship today is not "How much will we be able to gain?" but "How much must we be prepared to lose?" By common consent, the "free world" slogan has ceased to be expansion, prosperity, stability and progress for capitalism and has become the defense of "free world" interests against the expansive and explosive forces of nationalism and socialism. As colonial independence and socialist construction have expanded, the geographical area under capitalist control has contracted.

Meeting the communist threat to capitalist survival has been the chief preoccupation of the West since the war's end in 1945. In its earlier stages western policy followed three lines. (1) Stabilization, rehabilitation and restoration of the crippled and shattered Central and West European capitalist structure. Lend-lease and the Marshall Plan were steps in this policy. At the same time strenuous efforts were made to coordinate or if possible to unify the economic life of Western Europe under United States leadership. (2) Between 1945 and 1949 it was assumed that communism could be "contained." This containment policy was based on the theory that communism was an international conspiracy led by the Soviet Union, which could be brought under control by diplomatic, economic and military encirclement. NATO, the Baghdad Pact, the Anzus Pact and SEATO represented the diplomatic aspects of this policy. Trade restrictions, boycotts and blockades were some of its economic aspects. Militarily, it involved control of the high seas and the air, the establishment of a ring of military bases encircling the Soviet Union, the concentration of large military forces in Central Europe within striking distance of the Soviet Union and the reindustrialization and rearmament of West Germany and Japan as operational bases against the Soviet Union.

Rapid recovery of the Soviet Union and Eastern Europe after the war's end, the defeat of the Chinese Nationalists in 1948 and the establishment of the Chinese Peoples' Republic in 1949, the success of the first Chinese five year plan, the launching of Russia's Sputnik and the announcement of its ambitious seven year plan in 1958, the rapid development of Eastern Europe after 1956 and the turmoil and confusion occasioned by the spread of the independence movement among Asians and Africans, confronted the West with a stable, rapidly expanding coordinated East. A broad belt crossing the world's heartland from the Baltic to the Pacific was now occupied by avowed builders of socialism. The Middle East, Southeast Asia and Africa lay open to the communists. No longer was there a possibility of the West containing and strangling communism. The West faced an immediate and deadly threat to its very existence. Since containment had proved unworkable, the West turned to its third line of defense. The Truman Doctrine, announced in 1947, merged into the Eisenhower Doctrine as the inconclusive results of the Korean War showed the solid strength of the socialist position. A defense perimeter was drawn around the Soviet-Chinese area. Across this line communism would pass only at the risk of war. The issue had shifted to the question of Western survival.

The Eisenhower version of the new policy declared that any attempt to establish communism in "free world" territory (namely, beyond this defense perimeter), whether the attempt was made by invasion from without or by subversion from within a given country, would be met by military force. This policy was implemented in 1958 when the United States Sixth Fleet was moved into the Eastern Mediterranean and United States Marines occupied Lebanon to prevent a possible overthrow of the existing government. In 1960, with the Cuban revolution on Washington's doorstep, the Monroe Doctrine was applied to the interval organization of nations in the Western Hemisphere. Washington announced that an effort to establish a communist foothold in the Americas would not be tolerated. Moscow answered this pronouncement by proclaiming that any United States military intervention in Cuba would be countered by socialist military support for the Cuban revolution.

"Free world" nations, having lost the international initiative which they had held for four centuries while they were building the planet-girdling European empires, were confronted by an alternative social pattern. This new socialist way of life was neither a bad dream nor a mad-cap adventure, but a tough, persistent, expanding reality whose continued existence and growing power compelled the leading "free world" nations to alter both their domestic and foreign policies. Domestically, they have replaced 18th-19th century liberalism with 20th century fascism. The new pattern may be summarized under six headings:

(1) Consolidation of business, government, the military, the channels of communication and the apparatus of propaganda in the hands of a well-knit, self-perpetuating oligarchy.

(2) Assurance of comfort, security and status to the middle class, thus insuring its loyalty to the oligarchy.

(3) Provision of enough social security and other forms of welfare so that the masses will work and fight for the wealthy and powerful oligarchy which owns and manages the social apparatus and makes policy.

(4) Acceptance of labor union leaders as junior partners in the oligarchy and through them holding the masses in line behind oligarchy policy.

78

(5) Wipe out opposition. If possible, dissidents are bought at their own price. If they continue to oppose or resist, they are suppressed, using whatever measures seemed necessary.

(6) Denunciation and banning of teachings which call into question the values proclaimed by the "free world" oligarchy.

Internationally, the "free world" grudgingly accepts colonial independence and self-determination, attaching strings wherever possible. A significant test of "free world" attitudes on this issue came in the summer of 1960 when Belgium conceded independence to its African colony in the Congo and made a token withdrawal of its armed forces; then sent them back into the mineral-rich Katanga province. In this double-faced deal Belgium was aided and abetted by the United States, Great Britain and the United Nations organization.

Working primarily through its regional organizations, NATO, OAS and SEATO, and incidentally through the United Nations, the "free world" does its utmost to hold its colonial peoples in line and at the same time to contain, sabotage and obstruct the development of socialism. To do this it must keep ahead in the arms race and ultimately win the cold war, wipe out socialism and restore at least the semblance of monopoly capitalism.

General crises, arising out of war, economic unbalance, colonial revolt, social revolution and spectacular successes in socialist construction have forced the "free world" into a social crisis, with consequent insecurity, anxiety and fear of further defeats and losses. Under the plutocratic-military-fascist despotism organized in the name of freedom to protect the "free world" against movements for colonial independence and socialist construction, public policy has shifted away from freedom and has gone far in the direction of restraint. A glance at the formulators of "free world" policy will explain this emphasis.

The broadest common denominator in the "free world" is its anti-communist ideology. Until the beginning of the cold war in 1946, the Christian churches played an important role in formulating "free world" ideology. Generally through the years from the Paris Commune to the Russian Revolution the Christian churches were anti-socialist and fervent supporters of capitalist imperialism. Since 1917 they have been largely anti-communist. Christian churches take this position because for the first time in recent centuries their doctrinal thesis of joy and rest in heavenly mansions is being squarely challenged by a widely supported movement built around the assumption of joy and rest in a carefully planned, justly administered, well-appointed earthly home. The two ideologies are in sharp conflict.

Verbally, Christian churches (particularly in the United States) favor freedom and oppose authoritarianism and totalitarianism. In practice they are highly authoritarian and many of them are totalitarian as well. The source of their authority is found in the Bible, which the Christians hold to be divinely inspired. Although they constitute a minority of the human race they assume that they have the whole truth and that those who disagree with them are heretical or wrong.

Among the Christian churches the Roman Catholics have a larger membership than any other sect. Indeed, they proclaim themselves as the true believers and denounce their Protestant fellow Christians as misleaders. The Vatican, beside operating a church with some four hundred million members, rules over Vatican City, which is a "state." Through the past century the Vatican has been the leading ideological opponent of socialism and communism. It continues to hold this position not in the name of freedom, but in the name of the true faith.

The Roman Church is one of the most authoritarian and totalitarian of human institutions. Not only does it have the one

80

true faith but it is led by one infallible spokesman whose word is final in matters of faith and morals. Through its very large membership, through the organizations which it controls, through its spokesmen, highly placed throughout the "free world," the Vatican aims to shape policy and direct its implementation. On the issue of anti-communism, the Protestant churches have become a somewhat more liberal replica of the Vatican. Largely because of their fragmentation they are less influential in the determination of "free world" policy.

"Free world" advocates speak and write of their world as though it were unified, integrated, homogeneous. In reality, it is a loose aggregation or association of competing, conflicting nations occupying various levels of cultural development. It is neither a federation nor a confederation, but a grouping of five associations of nations, each held together by treaties, with no effective governmental structure. In the Atlantic area, the North Atlantic Treaty Organization (NATO) has a working nucleus made up of the United States, Britain, West Germany, France, Italy, Holland and Belgium. In the Americas the agency is the Organization of American States (OAS), which, like the South East Asian Treaty Organization (SEATO), the Central Treaty Organization (CTO) and the Australia, New Zealand, United States (ANZUS) organization are military alliances based on treaties, with a minimum of political structure and function.

Dominant in each of the five associations, and holding the "free world" together, are the wealth, prestige, economic, diplomatic and political activity and the omnipresent air, sea and land military apparatus of the United States.

Grouped around the United States in NATO are remnants of the European capitalist empires which conquered, subjugated and exploited the resources and labor power of Asia, Africa and the Americas. Empire-building and freedom are antithetical con-

81

cepts. During the past five centuries the dominant Western empires fought a succession of wars to determine who should grab and keep choice pieces of international real estate. Freedom is not usually associated with military conflict, conquest or occupation of foreign territory. "Free world" history reeks of restraint, coercion, compulsion. Currently, "free world" membership includes some of the world's most unsavory dictators and tyrants.

Representative Thomas B. Curtis, after an exhaustive examination of the "free world," came to the conclusion that it consisted of 71 nations outside the "Iron Curtain." Of these 71 nations, 49 were ruled by dictatorships or close oligarchies. In most of these nations the economies are controlled by oligarchies and "a small percentage of the nation is living off the backs of the 99 percent."[15] Mr. Curtis might have added that in the United States today little more than the shadow of political freedom remains, while the economy is directed by a plutocratic oligarchy.[16] It is an affront to semantics and an example of outrageous mis-labeling to apply the term "free" to the aggregate of oligarchies, monarchies, dictatorships and despotisms which are masquerading under the name "free world."

## 13.  EXPERIMENTS WITH FREEDOM

Any consideration of freedom in action should include some reference to the numerous casual and intentional experiments designed to enlarge the areas in which individuals or groups of human beings make choices and implement them. All such experiments call into question the theoretical bases of the established order, violate property law, attempt by extra-legal means to correct injustices and challenge deviations from the existing folkways, which are predominantly restrictive and coercive.

Folkways supplemented by legal authority have limited human conduct in many areas and over extended periods during which the practices of individuals and the policies followed by human groups have been determined to a considerable extent by tradition, precedent, custom and habit. Once established, both folkways and legal authority tended to persist, not only because children brought up to accept certain outlooks and practices tended to follow them, but because the community, acting through its more mature members, practiced the folkways, obeyed the laws, and did their utmost to have succeeding generations follow suit. Thus the folkways, plus law, became a social strait-jacket which imposed conduct patterns and restricted areas of choice.

Pitted against the arbitrary limitations of established society were two forces which led to improvisation and experimentation. The first force was emergency. The second was human imagination, reason and ingenuity. Emergency, due to natural disturbances or to the intervention of social groups, often brought the folkways, the law and the requirements of survival into sharp opposition. Under the pressure of over-riding necessity, the folkways and law were by-passed and new conduct patterns established.

Human imagination, reason and ingenuity, stimulated by necessity, came up with new ideas and action patterns which involved modifications of established social forms and procedures. Each innovation was in effect a declaration of independence from accepted action patterns. By replacing a less efficient culture trait

83

by a more efficient trait the group had won freedom (even if only partial) from the limitations imposed by existing culture patterns.

Innovations, breaking through established patterns of conduct, were in effect experiments with freedom. But the newly acquired culture traits in their turn imposed restrictions. The principle of leadership-followership among human beings is a good example of this process. The social group which developed the principle of leadership-followership won ascendancy over leaderless groups. With leadership came individual or minority direction of group affairs, resulting frequently in despotisms controlled and directed by individual tyrants or oligarchies. Most human beings during most historically recorded periods have lived under some form of tyranny or despotism. The overwhelming majority of the human race lives that way today. Individuals and minorities act against restraint, challenging their leaders with demands for greater freedom. Through such attempts at protest, resistance, rebellion and revolt, the dissident group wins temporary relief, especially if the representatives of the status quo are killed, jailed or driven into exile as a result of a political coup or popular uprising. By comparison with the previous period of established restraints the leadership of the newly-empowered group enjoyed relative freedom, but members of the group were subjected to the will of the leader, who was in a position to interpret and modify law and folkways in his own favor.

At a stage still later in the development of human society leaders appeared who rejected tyranny, denounced personal power and proposed plans for supplanting arbitrary rule by a united group effort to promote the general welfare. Manu, Amenhotep, Moses, Jesus and the more modern socialists were among leaders whose vision pictured a society based upon peace, plenty and friendship, in which all human beings would live

84

together more or less leaderless, sharing the good things of life, in a brotherhood of mankind.

In present-day socialist or anarchist terms this idea is called the withering away of the state. The concept is currently millennial, but if and when it materializes, it will be a virtually leaderless community whose individual practices rest back upon a degree of self-discipline that substitutes the individual acceptance of group decisions for the tyrannies, the rule of oligarchies and the super-imposed authority so generally exercised by the modern state.

Explorations and surveys of the earth's crust, coupled with scientific discoveries and technical inventions, have given power age men a range of potential control of nature and society that promise relief from the heaviest labor, presage a day in the very near future when, within reason, man will command and nature will obey, when social organization and administration will establish new levels of abundant, creative living for mankind.

Technical innovations enable men to dispense with established patterns and supply new means of controlling and directing nature and society. Each innovation which is adopted helps to free the group from past dependencies. Thus considered, a progressive step is one which releases man from the trammels of the past and opens wider opportunities for the future.

Many human beings listen eagerly to such glad tidings of enlarged opportunities for more complete living. The most venturesome and practical-minded among them invariably raise the question: "If we have reached so favorable a position, why not realize its possibilities here and now? Why wait? Those of us who see these possibilities should put them to work and set an example which our less imaginative and less venturesome fellows may follow."

During the period of written history countless experiments

have been made in efforts to liberate man from his bondage to earth, air, fire, water, the established folkways and the superimposed authority of the state apparatus. Local freedom experiments have been made through historical times by individuals (hermits, recluses) who tried by living alone to free themselves from restrictions imposed by society. Some experiments were made by workers in related crafts who attempted through guilds, unions or other forms of association to increase their economic and social stability and security through solidarity with fellow craftsmen. Saint Simon, Fourier, Robert Owen, Henry George, Tolstoi and other 18th and 19th century reformers tried to demonstrate their theories in intentional, planned communities. Some experiments were based on agriculture or trading. The majority were made up of individuals and families which had certain beliefs in common. Fraternities bound together in intentional communities by common religious beliefs have demonstrated greater survival capacity than groups having common economic theories and commonly accepted programs for social improvement.

William Penn and other colonizers of North America went to the new world fully prepared to establish communities based on truth, love, justice and fair-dealing. Penn was outstanding among these earlier planners of an improved pattern for individual and social conduct. He and his fellow Quakers went further than most other intentional groups in their efforts to combine freedom for individual decision and action with group leadership in non-authoritarian communities. At the center of his experiment Penn laid out his City of Brotherly Love, Philadelphia. Friendship, justice and fair-dealing in domestic and inter-group relations were to be the guiding principles of this libertarian experiment. At the outset Penn and his followers made friendly contact with the American Indians. Along a seaboard wracked by intermittent Indian wars, beset by fear and committed to the policy of "no good Indian but a dead Indian," William Penn and his fellow Quakers met the Indians in formal gatherings, dealt with them fairly, lived up to their treaty obligations and associated with the Indians on a man-to-man basis. This one colony at least was free from hatreds, fear and the dread of reprisals for wrongs suffered.

With free land and a frontier upon which the restraining hand of central authority rested but lightly, North America offered abundant opportunity for religious groups, like the Quakers in Philadelphia, the Catholics in Baltimore and the Puritans in New England, to experiment with freedom of worship. Elsewhere, intentional economic and social experiments were set up. In virtually every case where they were declared as guiding principles, pacifism was replaced by military preparedness, religious freedom by religious intolerance and persecution, and economic freedom by exploitation and monopoly. Despite well-laid plans, good intentions, and sworn pledges to set up and follow a way of life based upon freedom, justice, sympathy, understanding and brotherhood, most intentional communities established during the 18th and 19th centuries slipped back from altruism to egoism and from freedom to the forms of restraint which prevailed in the communities in which the intentional experiments were organized. Even groups united by rigorous, orthodox binding ties found it difficult or impossible to hand on their beliefs and practices to second and third generation young people who, with few exceptions, left the separateness of intentional communities for the greater security and comfort gained by conformity with the folkways and the accepted ideas and practices of neighboring families and neighboring communities. In some cases, legal authority was invoked to destroy the intentional communities and force their members to conform to the accepted norms of the surrounding society.

More general experiments with freedom have been made. The Indian Emperor Asoka attempted to raise his entire kingdom to a higher level of understanding and action. Pericles and his associates aimed to enthrone beauty, reason and justice among the peoples of warring Greek states. The European Renaissance and Reformation which led to the Enlightenment and the subordination of tradition and custom to reason, liberty, equality and fraternity were designed by their originators and advocates to replace the bonds of conformity by wider measures of freedom.

During the discussions which preceded the American Revolution of 1776 and the French Revolution thirteen years later, governments were established dedicated to the enlargement of life, liberty and happiness among men. The American Revolution, the period of chaos and uncertainty from 1783 to 1789, when the Federal Constitution was adopted, was animated by demands designed to increase freedom. Indeed, freedom, as interpreted by the more liberal republicans of the period, was to be the outstanding result of the long and costly struggles, first for independence, and then for integration of the dozen independent North American states into a workable federation.

The United States constitution was written to replace hereditary monarchy by republican governments popularly elected at stated intervals. This freedom of people to choose their governors, or public servants, was looked upon as a measure that would broaden the freedoms already enjoyed under Magna Carta and the Common Law by guaranteeing people the right to elect their representatives and to determine their own public policies.

Enthusiastic supporters of republican institutions, organized during the closing years of the 18th century, believed that freedom would be a remedy for the major difficulties which beset mankind. In France and Switzerland, to a degree, but in the overseas world especially, devotees of freedom believed that they had found a cure-all for social ills. In the United States they had won independence from the British Empire, but they had not abolished chattel slavery nor seriously modified property relationships. Outside of France, they had left large areas of Europe still under the domination of highly centralized states, governed by hereditary monarchies and aristocracies and by authoritarian churches. So far as Europe was concerned, monarchies and oligarchies were still warring with one another in their struggles to modify European frontiers and to win and hold mastery over conquered, occupied territory outside Europe. Political freedom, in the form of elected legislatures, had not seriously disturbed chattel slavery, serfdom, or the monopoly power inherent in the ownership of land and capital and the control of state authority resting upon armed might.

Modern experiments with freedom, historically speaking, date from the Renaissance and the Reformation. Politically, they date from attempts in free cities and West European states to work out satisfactory means for representing the forces of the rising business class. In the revolutionary period during the last third of the 18th century attempts were made to free mankind from feudal restrictions and to enable them to seek happiness and well-being in their own way and at their own pace. Colonial revolts, through two centuries, especially in the Americas, helped to usher in the "Freedom Century" during which mankind was destined to lay the foundations for the present-day "free world," —with the abolition of chattel slavery, the tapering off of feudal controls and the era of European imperial expansion. European free enterprise made the Americas, Asia and Africa a happy hunting ground for free-booters, plunderers, exploiters and colonizers, proclaiming the doctrines of freedom while riveting the shackles of bondage on colonial and dependent peoples.

These pioneers of a free society described freedom as a gift of God, an attribute of nature which was the prerogative of white Westerners. It was a quality without an opposite. Freedom devotees and practitioners could expect only benefits to flow from the extension of freedom. From it there could come no harm, neither to themselves nor to the larger community. Freedom was the philosopher's stone which opened the way to wonderful vistas of truth, order, beauty, love, sympathy and understanding. These assumptions were embodied in constitutions and other political programs. They were supported by cults and were presumed to lead directly into utopias. On the path to utopia freedom advocates conquered, colonized, enslaved, migrated, fought wars of imperial rivalry and survival, rebelled and revolted. The "Freedom Century" (1750-1870) was followed by the struggle to redistribute world power, by the suspension and near-extinction of freedoms during prolonged periods of warfare, by an era of fascist repression and conflict as capitalist imperialism disintegrated and decayed.

At least in theory freedom is experimental. Logically enough, freedom advocates devoted themselves to experiment in politics, economics, in the social structure on the assumption that once the bonds of restraint were broken and the boundless opportunities of representative democracy opened before mankind, the human race would enter the promised land. These experiments were made in many parts of the planet. They presented the blessings of freedom to people of different races and creeds. The results were devastating to the point of an actual flight from freedom into the safer haven of authoritarian, totalitarian, planned, disciplined social organization. If the numerous experiments with freedom during the past two centuries have proved anything it is that in the power age the path of advance leads not to greater freedom but to its opposites.

## 14. FREEDOM IN ACTION INVOKES ITS OPPOSITES

From its earliest beginnings, the demands, the achievements and the inadequacies of freedom in action have been such essential features of modern society that the terms "modern age" and "freedom age" have been used interchangeably to describe the period since the industrial revolution and the political revolutions which had their beginnings in the 16th and 17th centuries. Evidence taken from various fields leaves little doubt that freedom in action during these centuries met informal and formal opposition. The evidence shows further that freedom in action generates, arouses, invokes opposition.

Modern society therefore contains within itself forces of freedom and forces of restraint in a state of temporary balance or equilibrium. If the course of events moves toward freedom, pressures for restraint will increase. If, on the other hand, the course of events moves toward restraint, pressures for freedom will manifest. Consequently, a move in either direction upsets the freedom-restraint balance and stimulates counter-moves in the opposite direction. Swinging from restraint toward freedom during the freedom age has loosened the bonds of custom and habit in modern society, released individual and group energies and become a dynamic force which has upset the balance in nature as well as the balance in society.

Freedom in action has brought modern man face to face with five general principles which operate in human society as they do in nature. The first is causation. The second is the universality of dichotomy or opposites; the third is the far-reaching principle of ceaseless change; the fourth is the principle of change through sequences of cycles or spirals rather than along single straight lines; the fifth is the principle that action and reaction tend to be equal and opposite.

Thinking of freedom as the central objective of human endeavor, as the philosopher's stone which would lift all burdens and solve all problems, as the magic carpet which would bear humanity into the realm of pure delight, freedom enthusiasts overlooked historical experience. Worse than that, they flew directly into the teeth of the five universal principles of causation, of opposites, of change, of sequence and of action and reaction.

Proponents of freedom who were also students of the principles underlying nature and society might have learned after generations of experimentation that there was something amiss with their belief that freedom comes first as the solvent of human problems and the source of well-being. If they were not sufficiently advanced in their experience and study to be aware of the nature of these oversights, at the very least they might have been disturbed and disconcerted as they watched the transvaluation of their vaunted freedoms. Free enterprise in action became monopoly. Republics founded on solemnly adopted constitutions were converted not only into personal dictatorships but into arbitrary totalitarian regimes. Justice under law yielded place to rule by obligarchies which put their minority interest above the general welfare. Like every other fragment of human experience, these recent and spectacular shifts from new freedoms to new tyrannies and new despotisms are products of the law of cause and effect and are the logical outcome of forces set in motion by the abolition of feudal restraints in the era of expanding freedoms which marked the transition from feudalism to bourgeois society.

In its early stages the modern drive to freedom was directed *against* restraint. Its primary task was to break the bonds of tradition and custom that had grown up around the monopoly of wealth and power in the hands of landlords, warlords and ecclesiasts. This monopoly, once broken, released immense funds of individual and social energy which became a revolutionary flood of sufficient potency to upset the old social order. At such moments of overturn, power is disengaged, and lies ready to be grabbed up, like a fumbled ball on a playing field.

Revolutionary overturn liberates. It goes further than breaking bonds. It ends a cycle or an epoch, closing one door on the past and opening another door to a future in which old social patterns will be irrelevant and new ones will be inaugurated and maintained. It was conduct patterns and institutions that constituted the structure of the old order. Similar or alternative patterns and institutions will compose the new society.

Power loss by established vested interests releases volumes of unused or little used impulses to action. One of the first objectives of these released impulses will lead to the seizure of power which has slipped from the grasp of the old social order and its utilization to build an alternative social structure. In some cases, as in the Spanish overturn of 1932-38, decisive action by representatives of the old order may enable them to re-establish themselves after a struggle in which foreign intervention often proves to be the decisive factor. Power struggle, in which a previous ruling group or class loses its grip only temporarily, releases unused

93

individual and social energies which may be gathered up in the name of freedom and used to reimpose even more drastic restraints on the community.

Periods of social crisis and transition are accompanied by periods of maturation preceding the power shift, and of readjustment following the power shift. It is the epochs of maturation and of readjustment that really tell the tale. The power shift itself is merely the peak point on a cycle of social change.

Human society from 1750 to 1900 passed through an epoch which emphasized both individual and group freedom. The individual was to be free to act as his reason and interests dictated. The group was to be equally free to pursue its interests. The metamorphosis of freedom into its opposite—restraint—takes the same general form in individual and in group experience.

Important consequences flow from the emphasis upon freedom for the individual. Most apparent is its effect upon the volatile, self-assured extrovert who is ready to choose and act. For him freedom equates with opportunity. He takes advantage of the unsettled situation, pushes ahead in his profession or business, makes sound judgments, takes risks, garners one success after another. Relying on foresight rather than hindsight, he utilizes nature, takes advantage of the social structure and of his fellowmen.

For every dynamic, pushing individual who thinks on his feet and acts quickly and decisively, utilizing the freedoms that come his way and turning opportunity to his own advantage, there are many less dynamic, less aggressive who are acted upon. In a sense, they provide the social medium through which the dynamic few push their way to the top.

Some members of this middle group, observing the successes of the vigorous, energetic minority, are stimulated to join the climbers or at the least are carried along on the transforming tide.

Where the few take advantage of new-won freedoms to advance their own interests, members of the less energetic majority continue in the moderate group through which the dynamic minority is pushing its way. Thus the liberated community quickly redivides itself into the conquerer and the conquered, the initiator and the conformist, the owner and the worker. One takes advantage of opportunity to acquire wealth and position; the lack of dynamism in the other divides the community into those who exploit and those who are exploited.

Freedom to "rise" enables the few to push ahead at the expense of the many. To be sure, there is no sharp line dividing the two groups. Actually the energetic minority utilizes the abilities of a less aggressive middle group or middle class which plays the role of assistant, adviser, bodyguard or personal servant to the pushing few. In power age society this middle group is large, well-trained, generously rewarded. From its ranks individuals are constantly advancing nearer to the top of the social pyramid.

Those who remain in the middle class or among the working mass must adjust themselves to life in an ideological and social jungle, where they are free to act occasionally but are generally acted upon. They generate the mass energy which the higher-ups utilize to promote successful careers. They provide the raw materials out of which the higher-ups build their power structures.

Many individuals in the middle class (and still more in the mass) are frustrated and confused in their search for a rewarding life. Unable to reach the top of the social pyramid because of personal limitations or lack of social opportunity, they seek for security through conformity and through comforting contact with those who are in like case with themselves. Rebellion in their younger years leads to dissipation and hoodlumism. Disillusioned as they grow older, they go to games and shows, use narcotic drugs, accept crumbs of economic advantage and suffer from boredom, frustration and eventually from despair.

Emphasis on group freedom, freedom of association, independence, self-determination, sovereignty, leads to insecurity, disruption, discord, tension, conflict, insurrection, civil war, arms races, local and regional wars between armed states, general wars.

Individuals and rival groups jostle one another in their scramble for wealth and position. Instead of common effort for a common objective, each individual and group puts its own interest before that of the general welfare. Success is measured by the individual acquisition and accumulation of wealth, prestige, power. In this competitive scramble, individuals and local groups trample on and destroy one another. Local and individual success comes before the common good.

Competition therefore becomes the first principle of social action. Individuals learn to compete, become habituated to competition, and forget how to cooperate. Humans are capable of competition and rivalry. Some natures thrive on it. They are also capable of mutual aid and cooperation. Group development depends upon carefully planned, well-coordinated group effort. Both competition and cooperation are part and parcel of individual and group life. It is not a question of their presence or absence, but of the emphasis placed on one or the other.

While competition and cooperation exist side by side in individual and group life, the balance between them is likely to be delicate. It is comparatively easy to train a generation of young people to compete. It is likewise easy to train a parallel generation to cooperate. Emphasis on competition, once established, tends to perpetuate itself, setting up habits and points of view which stigmatize cooperation as old-fashioned, obstructive, subversive and therefore treasonable.

The extreme individualist is out for himself, first, last and all

96

the time, under the egoistic slogan "Freedom (for me) comes first." Thus the community is fragmented. Loyalty to a local group takes precedence over larger loyalties. Personal rivalries, feuds, factional squabbles and local interests attract attention, consume energy and wealth. The consequence is a veritable tower of Babel, in which men not only speak different tongues and elevate fragmentation into a primary principle of conduct, but in the end every man's hand is raised against his neighbor.

The process, beginning at the level of personality and local loyalty, leads to personal and local acquisition and accumulation of wealth and power. Human beings enjoying a relatively short life span are superseded by corporate bodies which live forever, acquire wealth and power, become vested interests and finally are institutionalized and become part of the structure of community life. Following the principle of competition on which these institutions were developed, the welfare of the part is put before that of the whole under the slogan "What is good for the part is good for the whole."

Opportunism, the struggle for immediate and local advantage, is the primary rule of conduct and is carried on for its own sake. The part not only comes before the whole; its interests and demands dominate the whole, express themselves in seizures of power, despotism, tyranny, civil war and finally destruction of the body politic. In the name of freedom men establish monopoly, oligarchy, totalitarian rule over their fellows, and finally destroy the community in which such divisive forces have been permitted or encouraged to develop.

Two sets of forces are at work in every individual and every social group. One set is centripetal, forcing toward the center, integrating, unifying. The other force is centrifugal, forcing to the circumference, separating, splitting apart and finally tearing the body into fragments. Cooperation tends to integrate and unify. Competition tends to disintegrate and fragment.

Differently stated, the human organism, like the body social, is subject to the opposing forces of integration and disintegration. Integrative forces construct and build up. Disintegrative forces destroy and tear down.

Individualism, competition and localism are disintegrative forces. Carried to the extreme, they tear the organism to pieces in the name of freedom. An integrated personality is the one in which the members, organs and faculties function smoothly, under effective direction. The same is true in an integrated social group. In a smoothly working organism, the well-being of the whole comes first. Only so long as the whole is functioning effectively can the parts hope for stability, security, development.

Freedom, individualism, competition are steps along the path from integration and harmony to subdivision, discord, tension and conflict. In the name of freedom, social bonds and ties are loosened, unity and solidarity are sacrificed, agreement and common purpose are forgotten. With the military occupying an important place in the determination of public policy, foreign adventures are undertaken, attention, interest, manpower and wealth are consumed in casual or prolonged wars. Disruption, bankruptcy and decay ensue. These social developments take place against a background of wasted and plundered natural resources, deforestation, loss of topsoil, flood, drought.

Power age technology steps up and speeds all of the social processes. Freedom of social action, in the power age, can lead almost overnight from self-determination and upbuilding to desolation, decay, destruction,—with the seizures of power, dictatorships and oligarchical despotisms that reach for power in every period of social disruption and disintegration.

Freedom in action tends to invoke its opposites. The more extreme the swing toward freedom, the greater the pressure in the opposite direction, toward restraint.

Reactions to freedom develop in successive stages. First comes pressure, followed by prohibitions. The extreme point of reaction is marked by coercion and compulsion.

Reactions to freedom take three forms,—contradictory opposites, complementary opposites and a headlong panicky flight from the insecurity of freedom to the security of custom, habit, folkways and common law.

Recent history provides significant examples of this principle. Feudal restraints led to the Renaissance, the Reformation and the Enlightenment, with their emphasis on individualism, natural rights and republicanism. The epoch of expanded freedoms, from the American and French revolutions to the close of the 19th century lifted freedom to fanatical levels at which men declared: "Give me liberty or give me death!"; "Though she slay me, yet will I trust in her." Foreign economic adventures, conquest, occupation, exploitation and expropriation of foreign territory during the freedom age led into the conflict, war, disruption, dictatorship, despotism, compulsion and conscription of the early power age.

Like so many social forces and relationships, the freedom-restraint balance does not stay put, but under appropriate conditions moves away from elaborate restraints toward freedom, while an increase in the number, variety and extent of freedom tends to move the pendulum in the opposite direction—toward restraint. Logically, a freedom age such as that which has developed during the past two centuries should lead into a restraint age, the beginnings of which have become increasingly apparent during the past four decades.

*Part III*

# The Freedom-Restraint Opposition

## 15.  FREEDOM, RESTRAINT AND SOCIAL
## STABILITY

Power age society is unstable. Discoveries and inventions, follow-ing one another in quick succession, have modified the life pat-terns of individuals and communities. Electric lighting has turned night into day and made possible twenty-four hour activity. The automobile allows men and women to live in one city and work in another. Air travel and radio communication have all but overcome distance. Automation has unsettled the labor market by displacing white collar workers as well as workers in shops and on assembly lines. In the West, rising taxes, inflation and the multiplication of debt, coupled with persistently recurring business cycles, have added to the uncertainty and anxiety con-cerning the economic future.

Politically the power age is even less stable than it is economi-cally. Human society, during the past half century, has been disrupted by colonial wars of independence, wrecked by inter-national diplomatic and military conflicts and torn apart by social revolutions. Scientific and technical advances which have raised the tempo of productivity have pushed destructivity close to totality. Colonial revolt, social revolution, wars with conventional weapons, and the prospect of wars fought with nuclear weapons and guided missiles, have further upset the social order and intensified the world-wide feelings of uncertainty and insecurity. It is against this background of rapid, widespread, unexpected change that we must deal with the problem of freedom in the power age.

Power age specialization, movement, insecurity and uncertainty all point toward conformity as the greatest of social virtues and blessings. A period of rapid social change minimizes the need for freedom and maximizes the need for restraint. Consequently the individual in his dealings with the community, and sub-groups in the community in their dealings with the dominant group, face the protest: "This is no time to raise minor issues. This is a social crisis. Sit down; you're rocking the boat." The richer and more powerful the dominant individuals or groups in such an emergency, the greater will be the pressure for assent to the wealth-power pattern and acceptance of decisions made by the wealth-power oligarchy.

Power age social groups which occupy key positions are keenly conscious of the dangers which threaten their wealth, prestige and power. With the aid of their propaganda agencies, their police and their spy networks, they are doing their utmost to hold individuals and sub-groups in line. The widespread nationalistic upsurge of the past century, the enthusiasm for mechanization and mechanical improvements, the demands for independence and self-determination, have alerted and alarmed the ruling oligarchies. Even slight deviations from the accepted social pattern which might lead to demonstrations and demands for widespread changes in social relations and institutions are frowned upon, prohibited and, where need arises, are suppressed by the representatives of power age law and order. The instability and insecurity associated with rapid change also offer themselves as easy rationalizations supporting conformity and arguing against deviation.

Whatever the explanations advanced to justify the widely current pressure for conformity, one incontestable fact stares modern man in the face. An era of unparalleled scientific and technological advance is also an era of mounting tensions, monumental destructions and haunting anxieties about the future. These catastrophic pressures, which are felt by the group as well as by the individual, manifest with peculiar insistence in the relations between the group and the individual.

In certain areas the group commands and compels under the imperative of "Thou shalt!" Perhaps the most widespread of these imperatives is "Thou shalt pay taxes." Whether the government requisitions are reasonable or unreasonable, whatever hardship they entail, taxes must be collected. Sometimes the taxes are direct, on person or property. At other times they are levied indirectly in the form of sales taxes, import taxes and subsidies. In any case, failure to pay is penalized.

Another "Thou shalt" appears in compulsory education laws. All children of certain ages are required to be in school. They may have no interest in or aptitude for book-learning. Parents may be out of sympathy with the school teachings. Neither excuse avails against the mandate of a law which subjects all children to the physical and mental discipline surrounding compulsory education.

Many communities believe that compulsory education is a necessary bulwark of community well-being. They may also believe in the value to the individual of disciplined indoctrination, which is the major function of obligatory school attendance. Whatever the justification, the community insists and enforces, leaving children and their parents the alternative of submitting to compulsory education or accepting the penalty of being haled into court, paying fines and going to jail. Recently, in a widely publicised conflict between a group of Dukhabors and the Canadian Government, the parents who resisted compulsory education went to jail while the children of school age were put into boarding schools as wards of the state and given the education provided by the school authorities for persons of their age and mental aptitudes.

Still another form of compulsion imposed on individuals by the modern state is conscription for military service. From small beginnings, the practice of conscription has spread until it imposes its "Thou shalt" upon millions of young men. No longer are wars fought between small armies of professional soldiers who volunteer for the job. Total war demands total preparation. Huge sums are voted for "defense." Millions are trained in the science and art of wholesale destruction and mass murder. As war becomes more mechanical, it requires more training before the prospective warrior can understand the mechanism, keep it in repair and employ it for maximum destructiveness.

Whether we review the compulsory education laws or the compulsory military service laws, we are forced to the same conclusion. Leading representatives of power age culture groups follow these coercive practices as a matter of necessity or expediency. The outstanding experiences of young people, born and raised in the power age, come from their contacts with an omnipotent state, with its multiple compulsions, backed by the force of public authority and usually supported by carefully cultivated public opinion.

For every "Thou shalt" which power age society imposes upon its individual members, there are a score or a hundred "Thou shalt nots." They include the prohibition of actions which are in themselves bad (arson, robbery, assault, murder) and a wide variety of actions which have been prohibited because they threaten the general welfare. Prohibited actions are designed to safeguard person and property, and to assure public safety. The multitudinous street and road traffic regulations which have been posted during the past half century are examples of such prohibitions. As government function has broadened, especially in the economic field, regulations necessary for the performance of these new functions have the force of prohibitive law. Municipal, state and national legislators are adding constantly to the mass of regulatory provisions already in existence.

Other types of prohibition have developed during emergencies. Martial or military law is proclaimed, and summary court martial supersedes trial by jury. Again, certain information is labeled "secret" or "classified" and may not be reported in the public press. In other cases, public authorities subject citizens to surveillance, to inquisition and to search and seizure, with or without due legal process. In all of these instances the individual is forced, under threat of punishment, to submit to prohibitions imposed by public authority.

Multiplication of regulations and prohibitions is the logical result of population concentration, community specialization, interdependence and the resulting interrelations of contacts and conflicts between individuals and other individuals, between individuals and communities, between private associations within communities and between communities represented by duly established sovereign governments. New York City, with its large, concentrated population and its multitude of municipal restrictions and regulations, employs an army of more than twenty thousand police, beside representatives of health, educational and other departments of the city government who see that municipal regulations are enforced.

There are many areas in which the group does not interfere by either compulsion or prohibition. In such areas, the individual is "free" to act. These areas, usually described as natural rights or civil liberties, include freedom of movement, freedom of speech and press, the right of public jury trial, the right to education, and adequate provisions for health. However, in human rights areas the courts have ruled that there is no situation in which the rule of reason does not apply. Consequently there is no such thing as absolute freedom in any of these areas. Free speech is tolerated until it threatens public safety. No member of an audience is free to shout "Fire!" in a crowded theatre. Freedom of press is limited by the law of libel. Freedom to assemble and to demonstrate are limited when public order is threatened.

Even in areas covered by constitutional, legal or customary guarantees of freedom, emergency situations are accepted as a justification for group interference with personal actions. Under the rule of reason, reasonable regulations and restrictions are imposed by the group in every case of a guaranteed freedom. Population concentration and the broadening scope of action by public authorities make it probable that growth and expansion of urban centers will result in more numerous and more stringent interference by the group in the lives of individuals.

Social pressures, forces and situations play an important role in determining the course of individual and social developments and the consequent relations between the various parties at interest. Bills of rights or lists of human freedoms are landmarks in social history. Certainly they have won widespread acceptance and support but, under emergency situations or in the face of public necessity, listed freedoms may have no more influence upon the course of events than brushwood along the banks of a flooded river has on the course of the stream.

Freedom as an implement or instrument is governed by the same principles that apply to mechanical devices. Individuals and communities which are able to make and implement choices and decisions may employ their freedom productively and creatively. Under such conditions crafts and arts flourish. The results appear in plans, designs, buildings, decorations, poems, dramas, musical compositions. Consequently, at certain periods and in certain places productivity and creativity move up rapidly to unexampled heights. Men refer to the Periclean Age in Greece, the Augustan Age in Rome, the era of cathedral building in Europe, or to the recent period of invention and discovery in the West as spectacular performances of a liberated humanity. At other times and in other circumstances, the course of events follows an opposite direction and freedom is regulated, restricted or denied.

Freedom varies in direct relation to group stability. The greater the group stability, the greater the freedom. The reverse proposition also holds. Hence, freedom is an opportunity enjoyed in times and places where public policy as interpreted by public authority leans away from restraint toward a greater number and variety of choices. A gradual or sudden change in the community power balance, coming from inside or outside the community boundaries, will be reflected in lessened or augmented limitations imposed by authority upon the individual. In this sense, under the most auspicious conditions, the freedom of individual action is an opportunity which may be modified or abrogated at the discretion of public authority.

## 16.  FREEDOM AND RESTRAINT IN THE POWER AGE

Our studies of the idea of freedom and of freedom in action have led to a crucial conclusion. Freedom by itself is logically absurd, socially dangerous and historically meaningless. The freedom idea becomes significant only when it is paired off with one or more of its opposites. We have selected one pair of opposites, freedom-restraint, as a starting point from which to survey the freedom problem in the power age.

The power age is a period of unprecedented concentration on unlocking nature's secrets, utilizing natural resources, more particularly the sources of energy, and constructing a planetwide social apparatus that will extract raw materials and supplies from nature, fabricate, transport and distribute goods and services, bringing to the humblest citizen advantages of which even the elect did not dream during earlier periods.

Construction of this power age culture pattern, its control and administration, have been made possible by widespread knowledge and understanding of both theory and practice, plus specialization, automation and interdependence, with resulting complexities of function which are as baffling as they are frustrating. Distance and time have both been telescoped, while the minute and the infinite have been brought within the range of comprehension, testing and evaluation. Through ages men used nature and employed association for their purposes. But only in the recent yesterday of human history has humanity developed formulas and techniques which have yielded mastery over nature and made possible the manipulation of social relationships with the same assurance that a potter, metal worker, sculptor or other master craftsman shapes and fashions the raw materials of his trade.

Power age science, technology, insight, understanding, mastery of nature and society have brought into urgent prominence not only the freedom-restraint relationship but the necessity of shaping and guiding social policy in a fashion that will assure the maximum advantage at the minimum outlay from the administration of the power age interdependent apparatus. Success or failure, the sheer survival of power age man as well as his further development, will depend upon the competence with which he handles the forces that make up the freedom-restraint balance.

Techniques developed extensively during the power age enable human beings to utilize, modify and, within limits, to control nature and society and to go and come geographically, socially, psychologically. Customarily we employ the word "freedom" to describe the outcome of these achievements. The use is inaccurate.

Men living in the mid-20th century are not free to avail themselves of nature's bounties nor to go and come geographically and socially. In both areas they must deal not with freedom, but with both freedom and restraint. Let us begin with timber, a widely available natural resource. In colonial days much of North Americ was heavily timbered. On the frontier, and in the Green Mountains of Vermont up to the last generation, when a native wanted groceries he went into the woods, any woods, picked the best spruce he could find, cut it, sawed it into proper lengths, split it into shingles, took them to the nearest general store, and swapped them for groceries. Today in North America and for many generations in most of Europe, such practices get the "trespasser" into trouble. Property law, with its side partner, the police, are the restraining forces. Indeed, the rising generation today, brought up in town and city, cannot even approach nature except in public squares and parks, or when vacationing. Nature is not free for them, but is fenced off by those who came, saw and occupied with the law's approval.

Or take the possibilities of going and coming, by train, bus, plane. If travelers have the price of a ticket, they can move about until they reach a national boundary line, with its migration quotas, passports, health certificates. Until 1910 it was easy for Europeans (but not for Asians) to go to the United States and Canada and settle down. At the same time it was easy for United States citizens to visit most of Europe. During the past half century, population movement in both directions has been sharply restricted. In many cases both entry and exit are limited by quotas, passports, visas and other legal barriers. Access to natural bounties and geographical movement today are subject to legal limitations under which violators may be severely punished. Access and movement are partially free and partially restrained. Property restrictions operate twenty-four hours of every day. Access is easier in time of peace; difficult or impossible in periods of emergency. In these two particulars, and in many others, power age citizen-subjects are hedged in by a limiting freedom-restraint relationship.

Mass production of automobiles during the first half of the present century offers one of the clearest examples of freedom-restraint limitation. Our family lived 14 miles from Mansfield, Pennsylvania, where there was an annual fair, lasting for about a week. Year after year we hitched up the horses, drove along the dirt road to the fair, unharnessed and fed the horses, met our friends and enjoyed the exhibits and activities. Nowhere on the road was there a sign regulating traffic nor a policeman directing it. We were free to go and come (at six or seven miles an hour) so long as we stayed on the roads. There was no direction, restraint, control.

Today, through this same Tioga River Valley, there are broad paved roads patrolled by town police and state police. Every mile of highway is marked out by directives and controls,—double lines, broken lines, speed zones, stop signs and stop lights, to regulate traffic which moves at a specified rate up to fifty or sixty miles an hour. Before a person can use the roads he must meet the legal requirements—buy a car license, take a qualifying examination, obtain a driver's license, and pay taxes on everything from gasoline and replacement parts to tires and automobiles. There is a motor vehicle department, with parking meters, traffic codes, traffic courts, fines, jails and other symbols of state power. In the power age anyone with a driver's license and a car license is "free" to drive—subject to a thousand and one restraints, at every hill, curve, intersection and settled area.

Productive capacity has been greatly increased by power age inventions and discoveries. Total product (gross national product) is divided among consumers (consumer expenditures), returns to the owners of the economy (rent, interest, dividends, profits), and government, in the form of taxes. Certain funds are allocated to production (reinvestments). Certain other funds go for destruction ("national defense" or war preparation). This complicated pattern of disbursement is not the outcome of a plan, but of an economic cold war, carried on through various domestic and international channels by the individual and corporate contestants for wealth and power. Eventually this division of income acquires the status of legal sanction. In the earlier stages of its development it was a battle fought by individuals, private associations, trade unions, corporations, government departments. "Free enterprise" is the name given to this jungle struggle for wealth and power. Today the struggle is "free" chiefly in name. For the most part it is sharply limited by the wealth and position of the contestants, and almost every aspect is subject to government intervention and regulation. Individual producers, consumers, managers, job owners and workers are about as free as passengers on a train, bus or plane, whose movement is drastically curtailed by the motion and the direction of the vehicle on which they are being transported. In a "free world" economy there are freedoms, but there are also massive restraints, prohibitions and coercions.

113

During the first half of the present century, technical freedoms such as speed and safety of travel and communication have been vastly extended. At the same time a network of legal restraints has been built up, so that instead of a "free" economy there is a freedom-restraint balance, leaning toward the restraint side as the economy increases in size and complexity.

Facilities for communication have been multiplied during the power age: telephone, radio, television, movies, improvements in the manufacture of paper and the techniques of printing and lithographing. These advances have been paralleled by ownership and censorship. The channels of communication are monopolized by means of property titles, patents, franchises, financial contributions. The so-called "free press" is far more free to advertisers than it is to subscribers, artists, writers. Artists and writers must be paid for their contributions. Subscribers pay only a fraction of the running expenses. Advertisers have big money to spend. Money talks. The channels of communication in the "free world" are for sale and are bought by the wealthy, who then proceed to dictate the way in which their property shall be used. There could be no more drastic censorship in a community divided between owners, hangers-on and workers.

Groups as well as individuals find themselves limited and restricted in the power age. Private associations may be chartered to carry out specified activities, subject always to the limitations laid down in the charter and to acts of the state authority adopted subsequent to the date of the charter. The association is bound by all state decisions unless they are invalidated by court action. Private associations, like individuals, enjoy a measure of freedom. Balanced against this freedom is a measure of legal restraint which operates continuously. Private associations, like individuals, may be subject to the restraining pressures of public opinion.

Public associations—towns, municipalities, counties, states and nations—enjoy a measure of freedom ordinarily called home rule, states rights, autonomy, independence, or sovereignty. As in the case of individuals and private associations, public associations are subject to limitations imposed by charters or constitutions, by legislative acts, court decisions, treaties and by the loose body of customary practices known as "international law." Since the drafting of the League of Nations Covenant, the United Nations Charter and the establishment of a world court, regional agreements like those designed to unify Central Europe or the Organization of American States, sovereign nations are restrained by legal or pseudo legal means. At the broadest level of decisions and choices, the level of international relations, a freedom-restraint balance exists. National sovereignty is subject to the check and double-check imposed by the foreign offices, executive branches and defense ministries of friendly and rival nations.

Freedom in power age society might be summed up in the formula: opportunity for those who are qualified to participate in a pattern of coordination and conformity subject to modification, without prior notice, in the rapidly changing structure and function of the economic, political and social apparatus.

In power age society, the pressure of economic and social forces, especially of technological forces, is toward restraint and away from freedom. With each increase in size and complexity, with each advance in precision, coordination and automation, the possibility of choice is reduced and the necessity for conformity to the demands of organization, mechanism and function is augmented. These limitations on decision and action are not primarily legal or political. Rather they are part and parcel of the rules of procedure if any complicated mechanism is to achieve the results for which it is designed and constructed.

## 17.  FREEDOM AND RESTRAINT OF THE POWER AGE PERSON

Freedom of the person has posed problems through the ages. Abstractly, the issue lies between those who hold that man has "free will" and those who insist that he is bound by his own past, by the past and present of society, and by nature, to such an extent that if we knew and could correctly evaluate all of the antecedent causes we could predict with mathematical nicety the next thought, feeling and act of each individual. Mortimer Adler and his associates devoted much attention to this problem in *The Idea of Freedom.*[1] The book is a dissertation on philosophical techniques, illustrated by an elaborate definition and description of the possibilities of individual freedom. We cannot review the argument here, but we can refer to the conclusions reached and the position taken by some of the freedom advocates.

Hegel thought of freedom as "self-contained existence." "The substance, the essence of Spirit is Freedom."[2] "Must the citizen, even for a moment or in the least degree resign his conscience to the legislature? Why has every man a conscience? I think that he should be man first, and subject afterwards. It is not desirable to cultivate a respect for law so much as for the right."[3] "The possibility of freedom is deeply grounded in our very beings," wrote John Dewey. "What men actually cherish under the name of freedom is that power of varied and flexible growth, of change of disposition and character that springs from intelligent choice."[4] Laski rhapsodised: "I am not a part of some great symphony in which I realize myself only as an incident in the motif of the whole. I am unique. I am separate. I am myself; out of these qualities I must build my own principles of action. . . . Their authority as principles comes from the fact that I recognize them as mine." "The individual, therefore, is entitled to act upon the judgment of his conscience in public affairs" and "to follow conscience as the guide to civic action. To do otherwise is to betray freedom."[5]

"The modern mind," Horace Kallen wrote, "makes freedom in and for the person the first and last thing; it takes all authority and all law to be secondary and derivative. It demotes them from powers that rule into instruments that serve."[6] It would be well to temper the exuberance of these protagonists of the uniqueness of human personality by referring to Whitehead's comment: "The human being is inseparable from its environment in each occasion of its existence."[7]

Water drops, assembled in the atmosphere and attracted by gravity follow a relatively simple course of action unless they are deflected or intercepted by some intervening factor. When water is free to fall, it falls. Human beings are in a very different situation. At the outset they are presented with two limitations, the human form, and the earth on which they live. Neither can be changed fundamentally. The complicated human being is composed of cells, grouped into tissues, organs, members. All are animated by life force, all are more or less interdependent. All are more or less under a central administrative apparatus functioning through the brain and the major nerve centers. In the face of these specializations and interdependencies, the human being is able to decide and act if the organism is functioning normally. In cases of subnormal or abnormal functioning, all bets are off.

Breakdowns which frequently occur within the human organism obstruct and limit personal freedom. The heart and the circulatory system enjoy wide autonomy. Digestion is likewise largely autonomous. If the heart is pushed too hard or if the digestive tract is asked to deal with indigestable or poisonous substances these organs function badly or not at all. The results are calamitous for the entire organism. The presence of too much alcohol in the blood stream paralyzes many bodily functions. One organ out of commission may deprive the human being of his capacity to make or implement decisions. In such a case, the individual does not do as he pleases but is limited by the inability of the physical organism to follow directives.

Other aspects of the human organism may present difficulties. Life force expresses itself as an aggregate or bundle of urges, hungers, interests, aspirations, all seeking expression. Frequently these motivating forces are in conflict. A youth, ambitious to make a good mark in his examination, is asked by his best girl to drop his studies for the evening and go to a dance. An athlete, faced with a trial of strength and skill, has a chance to overeat. Frequently humans are asked to choose between the penny and the cake under circumstances which deny them the possibility of having both. In such cases freedom is merely a chance to turn away from one course of conduct toward another course. Neither course of action may be desired. Both may be obnoxious, but stern necessity demands a choice.

Even the sturdiest, most integrated, most determined person is confronted by division and conflict within the personality. In the presence of dilemmas, the acceptance of one course of conduct usually modifies or excludes another. Under such circumstances there are many variations from rigidity through compromise, to surrender and perhaps mental or physical derangement. In no such case is the person "free" in the ordinary sense of that term.

Human beings face other limitations imposed by the web of necessity. The sternest of these is the time interval between birth and death. Before birth the individual is attached to another organism and cannot act freely. At death the human organism as we know it ceases to function. Since death may occur at any moment during the life span, each human being is faced constantly with this definite limitation on his freedom. Death might be described as an instant of total restraint insofar as the function of the physical organism is concerned.

Similar though less arbitrary limitations upon the freedom of the person are imposed by the disabilities of youth and old age. At birth the human infant cannot separate itself from the mother, cannot feed itself, cannot locomote. Gradually its functions develop and the child learns to eat, walk, talk, associate. But the maturing process—physical, emotional, mental and aspirational, takes many years. During this period personal freedom is limited by immaturity. At the other end of the life span similar limitations appear in reverse, as aging imposes structural and functional limitations upon individual action.

Physical incapacity during the period of maturity is a real limitation on the freedom of the person. The simplest forms of incapacity are the loss of members—arms, feet, eyes; the loss of tissues and organs; the impairment of faculties such as hearing, taste, sight. Beyond these losses stretch the wide ranges of malfunction or disease—physical, emotional, mental. Incapacity may be partial or near total. It is quite general in present day human society. Indeed, normal function is so rare that a vigorous, healthy, outgoing, normally functioning, mature human being is something in the nature of a seven-day wonder. From tooth decay, common colds and constipation to more limiting ailments, malfunction or ill health imposes varying degrees of limitation on virtually the entire adult population of a present-day civilized community.

Strictly speaking, if a man or woman says "I am free," the easiest way to rebut the rash assertion is to ask "Do you suffer from any incapacity due to loss or hurt of any members or to malfunction in any part of your organism?" If the answer is in the affirmative, obviously the boaster is in error in that respect.

There is still another area in which power age human beings are subject to sharp restraints. We refer to the adjustments that the human organism must make from the moment it enters power age society. The situations to which the human being must adjust include geography and climate, the culture pattern, the livelihood process (especially in its occupational aspects), avocational activities, mass living in all of its phases, and the immense changes that recent discoveries and inventions have made in the social pattern. In the power age the individual must adjust not merely to a complex environment but to one that is changing constantly. Adjustments resulting from contact with an environment in process of rapid transformation put a strain on human capacities that consign many individuals to the scrapheap before they have an opportunity to reach maturity. In no sense can these misfits be considered free. Rather they are the victims of an environment so exacting and coercive that multitudes are unable or unwilling to adjust to its demands.

In a chapter headed "What is Real and What is Illusory?" Horace Kallen noted that the restraints to which the power age person is subject may come from within or from without. "Of the powers that repress us from without, the most intimate are those of the family; the inventions of psychoanalysis have already made very familiar the mechanisms of family compulsion. Then in their order come the other institutions of society: the school, the church, the economic establishment, the state, and the general state of mind of the community as that is embodied in the accepted ideologies of the arts and the sciences."[8]

None of the limitations upon personal freedom that we have cited voids the possibility of enlarging the scope or improving the quality of personal life. On the contrary, limitations challenge the individual to overcome and to excel.

Each individual may aspire to live a more completed, rounded, satisfying life. There are four components in such a conception. (1) A life that will interest and arouse the individual, make exacting demands upon his faculties and capacities and stimulate him to his utmost in creative effort. (2) A life centered around well-defined objectives; a life purposed, planned, directed and administered with these ends constantly in view. (3) A coordinated, balanced life which invokes and involves the wide variety of human capacities. (4) A life dominated by self-direction and self-discipline, with awareness of possibilities and recognition of obstacles and limitations.

A self-conscious life is a project. Like any other project, it must be worked out as it develops and matures within the frame of reference that individual character, the personality and the environment prescribe.

Claims of the freedom advocates, like all other claims, are subject to the rule of reason. There is no such thing as a free person in the strict meaning of the term. Basic to human life are the drastic limitations inherent in the structure and functioning of the human organism. Each is at the mercy of the self, but in addition to self-limitation there are the multiple restraints imposed by Mother Nature and by the specific social environment in which the individual is entangled and embedded. Beyond the ignorance, stupidity, blunders and lack of consideration which each individual encounters almost every day, are the restrictions deliberately imposed by the power age environment. Among the factors in the environment restricting the choices and actions of the individual none is more restrictive or omnipresent than the authority of the power age state.

## 18. FREEDOM AND RESTRAINT IN THE POWER AGE STATE

Human beings structurally and functionally are not free, but are the victims of uncertainties, confusions, cross-purposes and inner conflicts that crib, cabin and confine them to such a degree that the term freedom is far from describing their lot. Like the poor cat in Shakespeare's adage, thought and action are both restricted, because they let "I dare not" wait upon "I would." Even greater restraints appear when we turn to relations between the individual and the power age group or groups to which he belongs, and by which he is restrained and coerced.

Since freedom is always tempered by restraint, there is no such thing as absolute or complete freedom. In the power age state the tempering process has gone so far that one might reasonably argue that restraint rather than freedom is its predominant feature. On this point Harold Laski wrote: "The problems of liberty in a pluralistic world are extraordinarily complex. The individual who seeks self-realization finds himself confronted by a network of protective relationships which restrain him at every turn. Trade unions, professional and employer's associations, statutory controls of every kind limit his power of choice by standardizing

out. When an individual battles against his group, he emerges, if victorious, not to freedom but to an uneasy truce which may lead at any time into another combat. In the long run the individual weakens, breaks down and eventually dies. The community usually survives the conflict and in that sense has its way, though its course may be modified by the stand which the individual has made. The word which accurately describes such a situation is not freedom, but conflict composed of successive combats.

Count Leo Tolstoi is a classical example of an individual in potential and actual conflict with his group. He was talented and had immense vitality. Until young manhood he accepted his place in the Tsarist social pattern and generally conformed to it. After some drastic experiences and much soul searching, Leo Tolstoi challenged the social system under which he lived to mortal combat. From that point until the day he left home and died in a railway station in his final attempt to win out against group pressures, his life consisted of combats with members of his family, with members of the neighboring nobility, with the army, with the Tsarist autocracy and with the established church.

Let us generalize this experience. The individual is in ceaseless contact with relatives, friends, associates, acquaintances. Beyond these immediate associates lie the less intimate indistinguishable masses who people the city, the region, the nation. The individual sees his fellow citizens as co-workers, as approving and upholding, or as opponents, as disapproving, as nuisances, menaces. The group looks upon the individual as a potential co-operator or competitor, a builder, a preserver or a destroyer.

Here is a confrontation that amounts to a contradiction and an opposition. The individual is one; the community is many. The individual is a newcomer; the community is older than the individual. The newcomer is trying to put down roots; the group is well established. Newcomers with considerable ability, bursting with energy and absorbed by the urge to self-expression, are face to face with traditions and customs established through generations and habits carefully nurtured from birth. The newcomer, even though a genius, is experimenting. The group is bulwarked, prepared, and experienced in dealing with dissidents and deviants. From such a juxtaposition various situations may develop: individual conformity and collaboration, questioning, opposition, tension, resistance, conflict, rebellion, repression, elimination.

Conflict situations involving an individual and a group present several possibilities. (1) The individual may win out and impose himself and his ideas upon the group. The normal consequence of such an outcome is a personal dictatorship or the imposition upon the community of an oligarchy in which the dissident individual or individuals play a prominent role. (2) The division of the community into factions, one of which upholds the dissident individual, with a stalemate leading to feuding, rebellion, civil war. (3) The group wins out, imposes its will and eliminates the non-conformist. Such conflict sequences have occurred repeatedly in contemporary and in earlier history. At no point does the word "freedom" describe the course of events.

Talented individuals who differ with the group to which they belong are more or less isolated and strategically handicapped in battles against the group. Ordinarily equipped individuals, possessing no unusual abilities or qualities, must accept direction or leave the group, unless they are able to establish themselves as members of a minority or faction.

Power age society likes to describe the normal, established individual-group relationship as "freedom within authority" or "freedom under law." Freedom within authority may be observed in the patriarchal family, in the established church, in the operation of customary or traditional status relations, in the role of the "good citizen" who knows the rules and keeps them. Some

United States Protestant churches are currently under attack on the charge of permitting communist infiltration. Anti-communism, a doctrine supported by the Roman Catholics since the Russian Revolution of 1917, and since 1946 accepted by the Washington government as one of the ideological foundations of the American way of life, is being widely accepted by United States Protestant churches. Under these conditions, freedom of belief is limited to those ideologies approved by United States secular and religious leadership. Actually it is not freedom at all but acquiescence and conformity to group pressures or physical and psychological bondage.

At the next level of individual-group relationship comes freedom under government or under law. Those who obey regulations are free to go their several ways and carry on their chosen activities or professions or enterprises, so long as they remain within the law. Power age governments go beyond this point by adopting bills of rights and other guarantees which (subject to the rule of reason and to some subsequent amendments or interpretation) are designed to protect citizens against infringement of their basic or "natural" rights. At best such rights or freedoms are attenuated, precarious, unstable. All governments in times of public danger may suspend the civil law (including bills of rights) under which these freedoms are guaranteed; may declare martial law, and concentrate authority in the armed forces. There are also possibilities, through a coup d'etat, that an entire governmental apparatus may pass from the control of one group into the hands of its rivals. During such turbulent periods it is customary to declare martial law or to set up a dictatorship or oligarchical authority that makes its own rules as it goes along. In the course of such an overturn, the old constitution and the old code of legal procedures may be discarded and replaced by quite different constitutional and legal restrictions and limitations.

Such sequences have developed in one modern revolutionary situation after another.

Another aspect of "freedom under law" cannot be ignored. Law authorizes and legalizes the status quo. Indeed, one of the acknowledged purposes of law is to define and promote the interests of which law-makers and law-enforcers are representatives. Laws made by and for supporters of the status quo are designed to thwart subversion and prevent rebellion. The slogan "equal justice under law" should read "equal justice for those who accept and uphold the law as presently written and interpreted, and subject to change without prior notice."

Wealth and power concentration; private property in land and jobs; wagery; monopolies through patents, franchises and special legislation; aggression, conquest, empire-building and the destructive and suicidal wars between rival nations and empires, all have had and have the sanction of law. Frequently they are blessed by the religious leaders and supported by patriotic private associations which back the status quo. In all of these instances the big guns, representing naked violence, lead the procession. The law follows along behind, agreeing, approving, sanctioning, sustaining and financing. At all stages in such a procedure, the law upholds the status quo and stigmatizes as subversives and traitors those who question and oppose it.

Since no governmental authority can hope to endure if it fails to secure or retain the backing of its constituency, law-makers and laws which support the status quo must adapt or modify the outlook of the citizenry to meet the demands of changing economic or political situations. Conditioning, in this connection, means establishing points of view, prescribing practices, building habits and customs that will serve the interests of those who direct the conditioning process. In passing, we would remind the reader that power age conditioning techniques, in variety and effectiveness, have had no parallel in written history. Given the currently available means of communication, a governing authority can reach its constituents at any or all hours of the day and night.

Restraints and coercions ordinarily imposed by power age states upon their citizen-subjects may be summarized in the experiences of a person born in a moderate income United States home around 1920.

1. Compulsory birth, expulsion from the body of the mother, with a period of adult-imposed hospital routine, followed by years of ceaseless indoctrination in a home where the child learns time-relations and acquires culture traits which are imposed upon all new arrivals. As soon as he is home-broken, the child is subject to the next stage—a space routine in which he learns the ways of the neighborhood and eventually of the town or city. The entire procedure, up to the age of perhaps six years, consists of the imposition on the newcomer of a culture pattern that he never asked for and may not want. It is imposed because the adult world considers it good for the newcomer and because most immature newcomers are unable to defend themselves against it.

2. Age six or seven brings compulsory education. Whether he likes it or not, and whether his parents approve or disapprove, the newcomer in a power age state must spend large parts of each year, for eight or ten years, under the disciplinary authority of educators who have been trained, conditioned and paid salaries by those who control the status quo. Their task is not merely to defend the status quo but by fair means or foul to prepare and train the newcomers to accept and support it. To secure this result the newcomer is given a place in an ant-hill school where he must present himself punctually, day after day. As a part of this routine the newcomer must go through a course of study designed to convince him that he lives in the best of countries and

should at call be prepared to give up his life to defend it. Year by year, promotion by promotion, he climbs up the ladder to higher levels at which indoctrination is intensified and elaborated.

Supervising this "educational" procedure there is a hierarchy of power consisting of a group of business and professional adults sitting around a board of education, a superintendent, a principal, and at the bottom of the motley heap a group of teachers who are perforce shabby, harried mouthpieces of indoctrination, subjected to incessant group pressures,—from the educational authorities, from the parents, from various pressure groups in the community.

The subject matter for indoctrination—the courses of study, textbooks, outlines and other data, are carefully prepared by specialists and revised periodically. Teachers accept the subject matter and present it to their juvenile charges. Failure of the teacher to toe the line and teach as directed leads to dismissal.

At graduation or commencement, the newcomer, now a model pupil, has been conditioned and prepared for the next step—to find a job and to become a model worker.

3. Job routine is less compulsive than that of the school because there is some choice among job owners, but jobs in an integrated mass production economy tend to follow the same general patterns. The newcomer is a messenger-boy, a handyman, or else he apprentices himself as the servant of a machine, which does much of the work and sets a pace which the newcomer perforce must follow. If the machine is turning out government orders, the newcomer will be security-tested to make sure that his ideas and associations are in line with those of his boss and his boss's boss.

The newcomer checks in at the beginning of his shift, to follow the job routine or that of the assembly line. As a model worker he may win promotion and preferment. Year by year he gains seniority. He hears about "management," but he is not asked to select his superiors or discuss business policy. He is a wage worker in power age production, the servant of a machine which operates from the lowest to the highest levels, wheels within wheels and circles above circles.

4. Conscription confronts the newcomer at some point in his school or job career. Whether he likes it or not he presents himself to the military authority for examination. If he passes the fitness tests he dons his military uniform and learns to become an efficient destroyer and a mass killer. The newcomer who was by turns a model child, a model pupil and a model worker, now learns to be a model soldier.

5. Model child, model pupil, model worker, model soldier,—throughout this sequence of disciplined controls imposed upon him (where necessary, by coercion and compulsion) the newcomer from birth has been a citizen of the city and state in which he lives and of the nation into which he was born. He learned about citizenship in school, sang patriotic songs and listened to patriotic speeches. He may have seen mayors, governors and presidents in person or on television, but the whole experience seemed far away and unreal. Now that he has come of age he can vote. For whom? Why?

Certain things he does know. He must not get tied up with communists. As for segregation, bomb testing, the North Atlantic Treaty Organization and the United Nations, better leave such matters to people who know about them. Discussion may lead to disagreement, to dangerous thoughts, to subversion. It is better for newcomers not to meddle in such matters.

Why should newcomers meddle? Are there not used cars in the lots, sports, television shows and the movies to amuse them? If newcomers want to learn what is going on there are the news broadcasts over the radio, which they can believe without questioning. What is more important,—supermarkets are full of food; there are clothes and gadgets to buy; beer is cheap, and new houses cost less than rented apartments. Thus it is easier and safer to be happy, have fun, acquire property and belongings, live comfortably, and let the higher-ups run things.

This, in brief, is the experience of newcomers into the chief power age nations. At every stage of experience from the cradle onward, newcomers are confronted with established facts and customs, which they are not supposed to disturb. The homes, schools, workshops, military establishments and police-dominated states are all set up and are going places. Newcomers who are wise will go along. Widely-publicised penalties for failure to conform are supplemented by the threat of frustration, isolation, perhaps incarceration. The individual who has his own best interests at heart will take the safe road, conform, and get by with the least amount of trouble.

Theoretically, power age law provides equal justice even if it cannot guarantee freedom. In practice the status quo monopolizes, discriminates, segregates. Established vested interests, private property, unearned income, job ownership and exploitation, nationalism, racism and classism are part and parcel of the power age set-up. Inequality and exploitation are built into power age society. The social structure is a pyramid with plenty of places at the bottom and precious little room at or near the top.

Throughout this pyramid, pressure, restraint and coercion are dominant. Freedom is in the background. Freedom slogans are formulated and fondled by academicians and mouthed by politicians, but they play a minor role in the life of Mr. Ordinary Citizen. In the power age, the freedom-restraint relationship of social structure and function have shifted far away from the freedom pole toward the side of restraint. Study any local social group; talk with any newcomer or mature observer, review your own life experience and you will find that restraint predominates and, from the nature of power age society, must predominate.

Harold Laski devoted a book to the role of the individual in power age states. "The unity of the state," he wrote, "is made by civic acceptance of what its rulers propose. It is not necessarily good because it is accepted. It is not necessarily right because it is proposed," but it is enforced in the name of necessity, defense, patriotism, and always in the name of freedom. It is freedom *under* authority.[11]

Individual-group relations in power age society are characterized by the dominance of restraint and coercion. In every phase of life there are broad areas of carefully planned social conditioning with narrow margins of individual choice and action. At every hand, in every direction, the individual is circumscribed, hampered and fettered by group restrictions which make him feel that if he questions, objects or refuses to be a good fellow and go along he will find himself a lone dissenter facing the compulsive power of disapproving thousands, perhaps of millions, including members of his immediate family, acquaintances, fellow workers and fellow citizens.

## 19.  *THE RELATIVITY OF FREEDOM*

Detailed examination of freedom as an idea, freedom in action, and the relations between freedom and its opposites leads to an inescapable conclusion: there is no such thing as a free individual or a free social group. There are approaches to freedom and withdrawals from it. Freedom is no more an independent quantity than it is an absolute. Nothing in our experience is total or monolithic. Life is multiple or plural—a mixture of varying proportions of various ingredients, of which freedom is one. Furthermore, freedom does not appear in nature or in society like gold nuggets in a streambed. Always it is accompanied by one or more of its opposites, such as restraint, compulsion, discipline, control. These opposites of freedom are generated by freedom in action,— each swing toward freedom resulting in an opposite reaction toward restraint.

Freedom is a relationship arising out of particular situations, each differing in degree, in kind, or in both degree and kind. Varying degrees of freedom and restraint are outcomes of these relationships.

It is possible to conceive of absolute freedom in the sense that one may assume an absolute vacuum or frictionless motion of material bodies. Practically, these conceptions of absolutes have no counterpart in power age communities.

Philosophically and theologically, freedom of the will has been assumed and discussed. Before, during and after such discussions, chattel slavery, peonage, exploitation, political despotism, war, conquest, empire-building, conscription, tribute, taxation and other forms of compulsion and coercion have been justified by custom, sanctified by the church, declared and imposed by law. Across the entire range of human experience there is no record of a situation that provided absolute freedom. In contemporary society, power age history is an unending sequence of multiplying restraints. Our analysis of freedom in action uncovered no instance of absolute freedom, but it did reveal omnipresent restraints, coercions and compulsions. Whatever philosophical or theological assumption and argument may establish in support of absolute freedom is contravened by past and present human experience. The practice of day to day living involves a sequence of limitations, obstacles, obstructions, prohibitions, enforcements, conscriptions and coercions balanced against man's multitudinous demands for freedom. This holds true in the life we live within our own beings, in the relations between the individual human and the social groups to which he belongs. It is likewise present in the relations between social groups. Nowhere, so far as our experience goes, is there complete or perfect freedom. On every hand, in every situation there are varying degrees of freedom and of its opposite, restraint.

Freedom varies in degree from age to age in the life of the individual. Newborn babes are drastically limited both in choice and action. Solicitous adults hover, decide, intervene. At birth the newcomer, however much wanted and loved, is a dependent inhabitant of a formalized, functioning, adult-dominated environment. With passing years, newcomer dependence decreases until with adulthood a degree of personal independence is achieved. The individual can now supposedly fend for himself. In practice, of course, the biological dependency of infancy has been succeeded by the sociological interdependence of adulthood in a complex social pattern. Actually the average adult is dependent upon more people in more ways than he was in infancy. As maturity is passed and old age takes over, dependence increases to the point at which the octogenarian, like the infant, cannot provide for his bodily needs, nor can he make or carry out the decisions necessary for his own survival.

There are moments when the individual feels free—when he is immersed in creative endeavors or listening to well-loved music; when revelling alone in a book, in day-dreams; when on vacation in mountains or by the sea; when sailing smoothly over the water or walking through the countryside; when in love or in quiet meditation. Temporarily unaware of time and place, the individual loses his sense of self and becomes one with the environing situation or with the infinite. Such moments pass. Coming back to himself, the individual encounters the same limitations that circumscribed him before his moment of self-forgetfulness or of ecstasy. Temporarily his awareness of restraint had decreased or vanished. The limitations remained.

Freedom varies with bodily function. In periods of normal function (health) the individual may be all but unconscious of his body. With malfunction (disease) the body may become an intolerable, torturing burden. The immense number of physical, emotional and mental stresses, strains, disturbances, disorders, contradictions, frustrations, identified and grouped by scientists, physicians, psychiatrists under the term "disease" provides a suggestive measure of the limitations imposed by malfunction on human health and freedom to choose and act.

Freedom varies with the social environment. There is a great sense of freedom with mother, with teacher, with friend, loved one, fellow worker. At times there is a greater sense of freedom when one is alone. At other times the presence of a group helps to remove some of the limitations which the human organism imposes upon the observer.

Freedom varies with income, wealth, social status. To a man in poverty, affluence may seem to equate with freedom. But the affluent face other limitations. "The only thing more cowardly than a million dollars is two million dollars," declared a multi-millionaire. The miserable sick king in the fable was told by his magician that he could regain health if he wore the shirt of a happy man. After much searching, the king's officers found a man who declared that he was perfectly happy. "The king wishes to buy your shirt," said the officers, "so that he may wear it and regain his health and happiness." The happy man smilingly replied, "I would gladly oblige the king; but I have no shirt."

135

Wealth and social status imply responsibilities and burdens. They do not insure freedom.

Freedom varies with the degree of responsibility that individuals assume and carry. How often we meet strong, upstanding men and women who bemoan their sad lot. They have a home, a nice family, a congenial job, a circle of friends and acquaintances. But they are neither free nor happy. They are tired of and perhaps bored by the responsibilities they carry, by the role which status requires them to play. You suggest change, vacation, travel, relaxation, play or rest, and receive the retort: "But I am chained to this desk. I cannot leave it, even for a single day!"

Freedom varies from individual to individual in the same family or neighborhood or work place. It varies from family to family and from neighborhood to neighborhood in the same village or city. It varies from city to city and nation to nation in the same historical period.

Freedom for one may be based on restraint for some other. Carl Becker's *Freedom and Responsibility in the American Way of Life*[12] reminds the reader that "the French nobles in the 18th century spoke of their liberties, but for the French peasant their liberties were oppressions, and to us they have all the appearances of unjust privileges." Horace M. Kallen quotes the saying: "The gentleman's sport is the workingman's crime," citing hunting privileges in Britain to prove the point.[13]

Freedom varies from hour to hour, day to day and year to year. The city streets, the water supply, the office buildings, while subject to wear and tear, are comparatively constant. Freedom to use them may be curtailed or obliterated by fire, flood, earthquake, civil war, military invasion, accident or police intervention. These are forces over which the individual has little or no control.

There is no such thing in power age society as total freedom.

Where some degree of freedom appears, it is associated with a reciprocal measure of restraint. The degree of freedom varies inversely with the uncertainty and insecurity present in each particular social situation. Conversely, the greater the degree of stability and prosperity the greater the probability that freedoms are available to the citizens of the stable prosperous community.

Emergencies arise in all communities. When threats to security do occur, freedoms are likely to diminish, or in the face of an overwhelming public danger to be supplanted by martial law. Flood, fire, earthquake, invasion almost automatically diminish the freedom area and replace it by prohibitions. Unanticipated disasters may reduce freedoms overnight. When such disasters occur, freedoms vanish like wooden structures in an area devastated by a conflagration. The freedoms are here today; gone tomorrow.

Similar changes frequently occur during basic shifts in the governmental apparatus. An old regime may be more arbitrary; a new one may be more liberal, and vice versa.

Freedoms may correspond with certain phases in the rise and decline of a culture pattern. They may be augmented during its expansion and may be drastically curtailed in the confusion and chaos which are likely to attend its dissolution.

Living and working in Germany during the 1920s we had many occasions to discuss the rapid rise of the Mussolini dictatorship in Italy, with the accompanying shrinking of Italian freedoms. Repeatedly, mature, responsible Germans (politically of the Left, Center and Right) told us: "In a backward country like Italy it is understandable that freedom should be restricted or even extinguished and that a personal dictatorship should be set up, but in an advanced, highly educated country such as Germany, with its great traditions of freedom and its passionate devotion to the liberty and dignity of the individual, such a transformation is inconceivable." The Nazi Party won its first significant electoral victories in 1927. In another three years it was being financed by German big business. Five years after 1927 the Hitler dictatorship had been established.

Freedom by its very nature is transient, evanescent. At times the transformations from freedom to restraint and from restraint to freedom are so unexpected and so rapid that they might be the work of a magician who puts a dove under his hat saying, "Now you see it" and then removing his empty hat, "Now you don't." If freedom were substantial and absolute, as some of its advocates would have us believe, if it could be established and perpetuated (as a course in music or a school of science is organized and offered to the public), freedom in this sense would be basic and tangible. But freedom comes and goes like the wind. Its presence or absence is felt only during and after the fact of its increase or decrease, after its appearance or disappearance.

In the face of recent experience and of historical evidence, we must conclude that freedom is not a substance but a relationship. The sun sets, twilight engulfs the land: it is night. Dawn comes, half-light, with the sun's rays on the horizon: it is day. So freedom is eclipsed by restraint. In another period, at a different point in the historical cycle, the social atmosphere changes and restraint is rolled back by enlarging freedoms. The sun rises and sets. Freedom comes and goes.

Freedom is an associational term describing the relation of one concept or one social force to another. High and low, cold and hot, rich and poor, are terms that perform similar functions. Each one of such a pair of opposites expresses a quality, but standing by itself, "high" or "cold" or "rich" is incomplete; the opposite term rounds out the picture. Our experiences with altitude, temperature and economic status lie somewhere between opposites or extremes. Like our experiences with freedom and restraint, they designate two poles between which individual and social action oscillate.

We have been writing about freedom and restraint as though these were the best pair of opposites in the field. But there is no "best" in such a case. There are several synonyms for "freedom" as there are for "restraint." Each one of the several synonyms has its more appropriate or convenient usage. During recent years the word "freedom" has been popular; in an earlier period "liberty" served much the same general purpose. Constant repetition of "freedom" in recent years has brought the word into a prominence which leads the unwary to attach to "freedom" a distinction and an importance which were accorded to "liberty" in earlier years.

Under no circumstances is the freedom concept entirely simple. Multiple experiences are associated with the antithesis between choice and conformity. One of the least satisfactory descriptions of freedom is the statement that "one man's freedom ends where his neighbor's begins." This description is based on the individualistic assumption that the freedom-restraint antithesis covers relations between merely a pair of individuals. In practice freedoms and restraints cover group relations as well as relations between individuals. All of the people in our neighborhood are free to drive on the street, to read in the library, to ride in the buses, to attend meetings of the city council. No one of these examples involves a confrontation of two individuals. In all of them the alleged freedoms may be available to all citizens.

In another connection, freedom signifies autonomy or complete independence. There are other dimensions of freedom in terms of natural law, conscience, social necessity. In any and all of these cases, practice will cross the boundaries which separate one type of freedom from another or it may include several of them in one experience.

Freedom is not an abstraction, nor is it a point or a line or a surface. Rather it is a many dimensioned figure, one or more of whose surfaces adjoin other figures representing other aspects of man's relation to himself, to his fellow humans and to nature or the cosmos. In no case is this simile complete unless, in every context, freedom is associated with one or more of its opposites, making the geometrical analogy far more complex and involved.

For our present purpose we shall be satisfied if we have established the relativity of freedom. Freedom, standing alone, is an incomplete term. To be completed, it must be related to one of its opposites. This relativity is expressed in the opposition and the reciprocity that is within the area lying between all pairs of opposites.

Freedom is not necessarily a good in itself. An overdose of freedom leads into license or aggression. An underdose of freedom involves despotism, domination, exploitation. The pages of human history contain examples of enlarged freedoms on one hand and of expanding restraints on the other. In terms of freedom-restraint as in so many other fields, the moving finger writes ceaselessly.

Freedom can be stabilized and can yield its maximum advantages in an individual or collective life pattern only when it is balanced against discipline, restraint or other combinations of its opposites. The result is an individual or collective life pattern in which freedom and its opposites play a definite but a shifting role.

Individual or group life patterns lie between two extremes—freedom at one pole, restraint at the other. In normal situations human beings never enjoy absolute freedom. Self-restraint and social pressures and compulsions are elements in every experience. Similarly, there is no absolute restraint, not even in death.

Similar limitations confront social groups. There is no absolute independence or sovereignty for a social group. Internally and externally there are oppositions, tensions, unexpected changes. Neither are there permanent restraints. Group life patterns, like those of individuals, are subject to ascertainable modifications and limitations.

Even the most casual survey of individual and group life in a power age environment will support the contention that freedom is not an absolute but a variable. One of the outstanding features of man's experience with freedom is its relativity.

*Part IV*

# The Role of Freedom and Restraint in the Power Age

## 20. *POWER AGE NEEDS AND OPPORTUNITIES*

Through ages of experience, involving manifold trial and error experimentation, various combinations have been made of the ingredients, natural, personal and social, which provide what human beings at various stages in their evolution have called a way of life or a good life.

Under the conditions existing in any known age, human needs have been numerous, composite, inter-related and interdependent. The onset of the power age has intensified every aspect of man's relation to himself and to his environment by making his needs more numerous, more composite, more inter-related and more interdependent than during any known period of man's life on the planet.

Since change is one of the most universal aspects of nature and society, the ingredients making up an acceptable life pattern alter constantly. Sometimes changes come so gradually as to be imperceptible to any one generation. Under such conditions of gradualness it is not difficult for human beings to adjust to change in the natural and social environments. But even in the course of a gradual modification of the life pattern, the ingredients composing it may get out of balance.

The loss of one essential part will throw an entire life off balance, transforming a workable, heretofore advantageous way of life, into an unstable, inimical one. Take two simple analogies. In agriculture there are several interdependent essentials: fertility, temperature, moisture, sunshine, thinning and weeding, tillage, elimination of crop enemies, short and long-range planning, effective management, concern and sympathy for the crop, constant vigilance and hard work. In power age society human beings desire survival, sustenance, status, wealth, power, stability, continuity, efficiency, economy, cooperation, stimulus, incentive, purpose, the will to improvement and achievement, freedom, restraint, a social sense, and a feeling of responsibility. In both agriculture and human life all of the elements in the pattern are necessary in varying degrees, at different times and places. Leave out one essential, even though it be a trace element, and the entire pattern ceases to make sense in the same way that an automobile complete in every detail, but with a short in the electric circuit, does not provide transportation.

Before we can determine the role of freedom and restraint in the power age we should have some concept of the distinctive features and the inner meaning of the age. Humanity's needs and opportunities in the power age are in many respects unique. Nations and peoples which have made the most extensive advances into the power age pattern of life face its problems more sharply than their less advanced contemporaries. Despite such variations the entire human family is benefited or harmed by one or more aspects of the power age and is concerned to make necessary adjustments to its peculiarities and its imperatives.

Americans are well aware of power age demands, requirements and limitations because the United States and Canada (and to a rapidly increasing extent the industrial areas of Latin America) have been transformed in two or three generations from handcraft economies, horse-and-buggy transportation and cash-box accounting into an age of mass production, electrification, automation, auto, truck and plane transportation, accounting, cost-keeping and auditing by automatic business machines, and economic-social planning on a nationwide and international plane. The entire economic and social structure of the mid-19th century had been abandoned or modernized by the 1950s. The transforming process is still moving along at breath-taking speed. This combined economic and social revolution has ushered in the power age, presenting mankind with increasingly insistent problems, several of which are important in any consideration of power age needs and opportunities.

1. Rapid extension of human understanding and control of nature and her resources, particularly of her sources of energy. Expansion of the natural sciences, astronomy, physics, chemistry, geology, metallurgy, electronics, atomics, biology, genetics. Development of engineering and technology in these and related fields. In the past hundred years there have been more significant discoveries and inventions than in the previous thousand years. Mankind is literally snowed under by the abundance and variety of the new knowledge and its multiple intrusion into everyday affairs. We may reasonably ask "Why this plenitude of invention and discovery at this time?" without expecting a definitive answer. Whether we know the cause or not we must face the consequences of abundant production, speedy transportation, instantaneous communication, a vast extension of social services and the possibilities of greatly extended leisure.

2. Application of scientific and engineering techniques, developed and expanded in dealings with nature, to include the direction and administration of human society. Planning, control and direction are not new. They date back to the planning of cities, harbors, waterworks, the organization of governments,

the assembling of man-power for construction, and for war. Written history reports these and many other examples of planning, control and administration in certain river valleys and on certain islands or peninsulas. But it has remained for power age man, equipped by science and technology with improved means of production, construction, transportation and communication, to bring under his direct control the social apparatus of entire continents with hundreds of millions of inhabitants, and incidentally, to plan, organize and control the entire apparatus of human culture currently existing on the planet. Power age man has gone further, modifying and renovating established social systems, and conceiving, designing, planning and building new social patterns within a single generation. While natural science and engineering date back through many centuries, social science and engineering are to a large extent products of the power age.

3. Natural science and engineering, coupled with social science and engineering, have unified or worldized the planet. Previous civilizations have been confined to a single river valley and its adjacent territory, to a particular region or continent. Mountains, deserts and oceans effectively separated and isolated them from contemporary human societies. It has fallen to the lot of western civilization, with its proliferation of science and technology in many fields, to leap over natural obstacles and integrate the present planetwide culture pattern. For the first time in written history, all men, everywhere on the planet, are pooling their scientific and technical know-how and engaging in various common enterprises dealing with travel, communication, commerce, exploitation, health, the weather, and other areas of worldwide cultural interchange.

4. Power age science and technology have enabled mankind to enter space, beyond the earth's atmosphere and gravitation field, and to study and investigate the moon, other planets, the

planetary system, and other stars with their satellites. In addition to probing outer space, power age man is developing the possibility of travelling to other celestial bodies, exploring them, associating with their inhabitants, establishing diplomatic relations and cultural exchanges with them, while maintaining a becoming sense of proportion and a feeling of humility in the presence of so magnificent an experience as a close-up glimpse of the manifested universe.

5. Science and technology have made possible the prolonging and enriching of human life, enabling men, through the study of biology, psychology, sociology, cosmology, to realize the good life personal, to work toward the good life social and contribute to the good life universal.

6. Destructive potentials exist in scientific and technical discoveries and inventions. Physics, chemistry, biology, sociology and psychology, applied to everyday personal, social and cosmic affairs, may extend, augment, enhance and enrich human life. The same potentials, turned from production to destruction, may cramp, hamper, cripple and terminate human life. Philosophers and moralists assure us that the higher we climb the farther we may fall. Every tool is a potential weapon, as every weapon is a potential tool. The capacity to produce and build carries with it the possibility of tearing down and destroying. During recent decades destructivity has advanced more rapidly than productivity. With the developments in atomics, chemistry and biology, projects, enterprises and culture patterns that have been built through centuries can be blasted, poisoned or mutated out of existence while these words are being read. Western man, having climbed far and high, finds himself hanging over a chasm of potential annihilation. Either he will control the forces which his discoveries and inventions have called into being, or they will exterminate him.

149

7. Faced by the challenge of this untoward opportunity, power age man must dedicate his energies, his new knowledge, his newly acquired techniques and his as yet little understood potentialities to building up the creative powers of humanity and thus participating, however minutely, in the expansion, improvement and the ultimate perfection of the good life universal.

These seven assumptions or axioms covering some of the major problems of the power age should be supplemented by an eighth —applicable to this and every other age. Power age life is so complex and complicated and its many fields are so highly specialized that it is difficult for people generally to be moderately well-informed as to the course and trend of events. Special efforts therefore are in order to keep the masses of people adequately and accurately briefed, not only on day-to-day occurrences (news in the best sense) but on the possibilities of building these newly acquired potentials into a revamped environment in which problems of general concern are foreseen before they arise and are dealt with by preventive rather than curative measures.

If these propositions correctly describe the needs and opportunities which challenge power age humanity, they warrant two basic assumptions regarding the freedom-restraint juxtaposition. From the viewpoint of the group or community (the human family), purpose, plan, control, cooperation, coordination and direction hold the same position of importance that they do in any group projects such as conserving, utilizing and economizing natural resources or developing an educational program that will prepare the next generation of human beings for successful and effective participation in expanding and enriching power age life. If the power age community is to survive and to progress, the conservation and utilization of nature, the planned direction of social forces, the development of world awareness and world loyalty, space communication and association, the prolongation and enrichment of human life and the development of human creativity must enjoy top priority in power age thinking, planning and performance.

Conditions, situations and problems confronting power age man are increasingly social in the sense that they concern larger areas of geography and population and can be more successfully dealt with by the group than by the individual. While the individual has a role to play in every life experience, the major fields outlined above are primarily "We" problems and only incidentally "I" problems. With the rapid maturing of power age culture during the last half century, the "We" aspects of life have not only pushed to the center of the stage, but they have grown in complexity, in intensity and in geographical magnitude. The argument presented in the last few paragraphs is more pertinent and imperative today than it was fifty years ago. Power age development is pushing life rapidly in the "We" direction.

Pursuing policies which demand increasing priority of "We-ness" over "I-ness," power age men must be prepared to work and live increasingly as members of closely integrated teams and coordinated groups. Group work and group life involve varying degrees of restraint,—both self-restraint and restraints imposed upon the individual by the group in its corporate capacity. Under such conditions, "We-ness," with its demands for group function, must take precedence over "I-ness," with its demands for personal self-expression. Major power age developments are progressively subordinating freedom and giving priority to restraint.

The second generalization complements the first. From the viewpoint of the individual, health, self-expression, balanced living, growth, order, beauty, love, recognition, approval and a sense of responsibility to the community are desirable and necessary. The achievement of these individual objectives will make the individual who attains them not only an adjusted, happy person, but a more useful and effective member of the group or groups to which he belongs. Individual incentive and freedom to strive are essential elements in the power age pattern, but emphasis should be laid upon team discipline, dedication and achievement rather than upon the freedom of the individual to go his own way, at his own pace, determined by his personal wishes and inclinations.

Power age requirements do not call for a choice between the group and the individual. The group and the individual are inter-connected and inter-dependent in the power age as in any other stage of social development. An individual cannot meet power age problems alone. He must participate with others in work, study, research, the formulation of plans and projects and their fulfillment in increased general welfare. As the group grows in size and advances toward automation in technology, the individual acts less and less as a person and more and more as a member of a team. Some of these associations are voluntary in the sense that the decision as to membership rests with the individual. Others, like citizenship in a state or activity in the armed forces, are based on coercion. In either case, once membership on the team or in the group has been established, group pressure plays so large a role in holding the individual in line that the chances favor conformity to group requirements rather than conduct determined by the individual in terms of his own desires and decisions.

Under these changing and maturing conditions values must be weighed and priorities established. Ardent freedom advocates take it for granted that in working out such a project, freedom comes first. "Freedom is not a luxury that we can indulge in when at last we have security and prosperity and enlightenment," wrote Henry Commager. "It is rather antecedent to all of these, for without it we can have neither security nor prosperity nor enlightenment." "We must preserve and encourage the essence of freedom of inquiry, investigation, dissent, association, education, science, literature, politics, freedom, in short, in all of its manifestations not as an abstract right but an imperative necessity."[1]

Underlying this program is the assumption that power age man is able to decide, choose and act. Unquestionably he has been liberated, says Erich Fromm, "from the external bonds that would prevent him from doing and thinking as he sees fit. He would be free to act according to his own will if he knew what he wanted, thought and felt. But he does not know. He conforms to anonymous authorities and adopts a self which is not his. The more he does this, the more powerless he feels, the more is he forced to conform. In spite of a veneer of optimism and initiative, modern man is overcome by a profound feeling of powerlessness which makes him gaze toward approaching catastrophes as though he were paralyzed."[2]

We agree with Professor Commager that freedom is imperative, but we would like to ask him three questions: (1) Are other power age objectives also imperative? (2) Are there any conditions under which an objective such as survival or improvement becomes more imperative than freedom? (3) Are not security, prosperity, enlightenment and freedom interdependent means to human advancement?

Faced with the frailties and contradictions besetting western civilization in the mid-20th century, we should be inclined to rate social objectives in this order of importance: *first,* justice, including economic justice; *second,* order and balance; *third,* peace; *fourth,* freedom. When the current crisis has been resolved there will be rearrangements of the priority scale. For the duration of the crisis this priority pattern seems likely to result in the greatest advantage to the greatest number.

On the frontier, in the early stages of any enterprise, the assertive, aggressive, venturesome individual was at a premium because he was able to act and survive "on his own." In the power age, the individual who seeks to act on his own as a free enterpriser is at a serious disadvantage. He may be obstructive. In whatever direction he turns he encounters group instructions and directives. His ability to understand the instructions and to carry out the directions determine his value as a member of the group.

Effectiveness, in a large, complex interdependent group, requires planning, technical training, coordination, cooperation, discipline, discussion, evaluation and group decisions in which individuals participate and concur.

Since the individual cannot establish or carry on a power age community, the survival and the success of the group are preconditions of the well-being of its members. While group survival and effectiveness are necessary, the individual is expendable, since any person with the requisite training and experience may take the place of an absent team-mate. The removal of one personality need not decrease the effectiveness of the team. Hence, in the name of the general welfare, group survival must have priority over individual wishes or requirements. There is nothing new in this principle. One of the axioms of social organization is that in an emergency or in case of a deadlock, the well-being of the whole team must be considered before that of any of its members.

Under power age conditions group equilibrium and stability are necessary for group survival and improvement. This is true of local power age groups. It is likewise true for larger groups, up to and including the human race.

## 21. GROUP FREEDOM AND RESTRAINT IN THE POWER AGE

Human experience falls into two broad categories—I-ness and We-ness. I-ness refers to the individual, in his relations with himself and in his contacts with one or more social groups. We-ness refers to human groups in their relations with individuals and with other groups.

I-ness, theoretically and in practice, is generally understood as the cult of the individual, or individualism, which has played so prominent a role in the recent history of western civilization. As a consequence of this cult, successive generations have taken it for granted that ultra-individualism is the norm of human nature and one of the significant objectives of social endeavor.

Nevertheless human beings, even those reared and conditioned in accordance with the cult of individualism, practice We-ness as well as I-ness. They do this, not as a result of theory, but as a matter of necessity. The human family is an example of We-ness just as each individual is an example of I-ness. "Few men can find a meaning in their lives unless they identify themselves with others whose purposes they share. And while they are urgently seeking to establish this sense of common purpose, the man who demands to go his own way seems a traitor."[3]

Human beings are persistently and insistently individual. Self-awareness and the pressure of urges and desires lead toward individual self-assertion. Reading the utterances of aggressive individuals and hearing them talk, one is tempted to conclude that this is the outstanding human characteristic. Certainly it is the outstanding quality of self-assertive vocal egoists.

Most humans are neither self-assertive nor vocal, nor are they outstandingly egoistic. On the contrary, they seek and find their satisfactions as members of one or more social groups. Their dominant characteristic is their eagerness to join the crowd. A few human beings express themselves by standing out from the crowd. The great majority of adult men and women stay with the crowd. They are persistently and insistently social. For them the coveted life-norm is the anonymity of the good-mixer who joins up with any crowd, becomes part of it and goes along with it. The name given to this social instinct or social sense is gregariousness—going together and staying together in groups.

Ashley Montague goes further. "Every person is socially bound to the group in which he has been socialized. In this sense the 'individual' is a myth. From the standpoint of the social situation there are no individuals, except as abstracted biological entities or for the quantative purposes of a census."[4] This conception definitely subordinates I-ness to We-ness.

Human beings have no monopoly of gregariousness or sociality. Many other animals, insects, birds and fishes display the same sense of We-ness. They get together and stay together. Our present purpose is to designate We-ness as one of the essential aspects of human nature, and then to point out that the coordination, specialization, interdependence and mass living, which are among the most prominent aspects of power age society, are expressions of We-ness.

Human groups, from the family and the neighborhood to the city, the region, the state and the nation, are aggregates of individuals held together by various bonds—biological, emotional, economic, social. If they are to persist, human groups must discover or build up common interests, ideas, purposes, practices. Structurally, group life tends to follow functional lines. People seek out fellow humans with like interests. Craftsmen, business-men, nature lovers, sportsmen, musicians, artists join others with similar inclinations or proclivities. Those engaged in the same occupations, trades, professions and avocations tend to associate and congregate.

Human societies are not monoliths. On the contrary, families are merged in neighborhoods and neighborhoods in larger group-ings. Cities and nations do not consist of individuals, but are structures composed of public and private subgroups, families, neighborhood, towns, cities, and the numerous private associa-tions which play so large a role in power age communities.

Group forms and group practices vary widely, but there are two features of group life that are all but universal: (1) insistence that the component elements of the group stay in the group and remain loyal to it, and (2) solidarity in defending and promoting group interests. These two principles of loyalty and solidarity exist in lesser or greater degree in all human communities. It is probable that the success of any human group in establishing, perpetuating and developing itself is determined in large part by loyalty and solidarity. Initially, personal leadership is a major factor in building human society. In the power age, however, the task of establishing the group has been far advanced. Power age groups face three major problems—survival, defense, and development.

As power age groups tend to be geographically extensive and numerically large, the members of a power age community can-not all meet and talk at once. They must select or accept their spokesmen and depend upon them to uphold and advance the interests of the group. In the long run these spokesmen tend to be the aggressive, vocal, egoistic members of the group. Through generations of trial and error the modern nation has evolved as the climax structural expression of group needs.

Sovereignty is the characteristic feature of power age nations.

Sovereign actually means "knowing no master." A sovereign individual rules over his subjects. A sovereign state determines its own policies, carries out its own practices and moves toward its own destiny, untrammeled, unrestricted, uncoerced. A sovereign state is a free state in the classic meaning of the word "free." Therefore our discussion of group freedom in the power age begins quite logically with the sovereign or free state, the form of association under which power age society is proceeding to the fulfilment of its destiny.

Our discussion of the relation of the individual to power age society has prepared us to accept the proposition that in the power age the group is master and the individual is vassal, enjoying those examples of the good things of life which keep him a model worker during peacetime and a model soldier in epochs of military struggle. The power age state formulates its own patterns for survival, security and development. The newcomer is fitted into the patterns with a minimum of friction and a maximum of ease and satisfaction for the state, and hopefully also for the individual.

By way of assuring survival, defense and development, the sovereign state expects the individual to be loyal (patriotic); to go through years of compulsory indoctrination in schools maintained for this purpose by the state; to accept compulsory training and military service even at the cost of life itself; to pay taxes as and when determined by the oligarchy which makes and implements public policy; to recognize the right of eminent domain, under which private property may be taken for public uses with or without the consent of the owner. If at any point in this unbroken line of indoctrination, persuasion, compulsion and coercion the individual questions, resists or rebels he may be deprived of his job and his livelihood, deprived of his freedom and stuffed into jail or concentration camp, or, if state security requires it, the individual may be deprived of his life. Under the conditions prevailing in power age society, sovereignty for the group requires obedience and conformity of its individual members. If the individual asserts his individuality and refuses to go along with state policy, the state restrains, coerces, and in extreme cases, liquidates the individual in the interest of survival, defense and public welfare. Under these conditions, restraint is predominant; freedom is subordinate.

National sovereignty (or freedom of the group to act in the interest of its own survival, defense and development) has two aspects—one, its relations with its own citizen-vassals; the other, its relations with other sovereign states. In the power age there are upwards of one hundred sovereign nations, either adjacent to one another or in daily contact with one another. The principle of sovereignty (group freedom of action) presupposes the right of each nation to defend and advance its own interests and those of its citizen-subjects. Is this assumption of group freedom to deal with other groups as nebulous and as inaccurate as the assertion that individual freedom is a dominant feature of the power age?

There are no two opinions about the principles of sovereignty. When a nation declares its independence and institutes its own political and economic pattern it is a sovereign member of the family of nations. Thenceforth it promotes its own interests by economic, political, and where necessary, by military means.

Another principle enters the scene at this point, supplementing and modifying the principle of sovereignty—the principle of competition. If each nation is free to defend and promote its own interests and those of its citizen-subjects, and if two or more of the parties at interest set out to reach a given objective at the same time, there will be a collision and probably a conflict, from which one party will emerge with the coveted prize, while the loser comes out empty-handed, or, if defeated in military combat, may be stripped of transportable possessions, saddled with indemnities or even dismembered and parcelled out among the victors. All three of these results followed the wars of 1914 and 1939. Actually, this is a thumbnail sketch of the history of recent centuries during which sovereign states were assuming their present forms. Within its own borders, the state could deal with its citizen-subjects pretty much as it chose, unless rebellion or revolution intervened. But in its dealings with other states the principle of competition limited its actions and often, if it were defeated, extinguished its sovereignty.

Power age nations have relied in their development upon the threat of armed force and the use of armed force. Their survival and development have been the outcome not of freedom, but of their ability to impose their will upon their neighbors, where necessary as a result of military combat, in which the victor compels the vanquished to do his will.

History, in the power age, has been made not by the free action of sovereign states, but by the outcome of struggles between representatives of rival states who sought to promote the interests of their respective nations at the expense of rivals under the competitive precept: "Let him take who has the power, and let him keep who can." It was under the aegis of this precept that the planet-wide 19th century empires were built.

National sovereignty (freedom of the group) has been subordinated to the game of international grab-and-keep. Only the winner in the game can pretend to sovereignty. The losers are forced to the winner's demands. They may be annexed by the winner or they may become dependencies of the winner. This game, commonly called power politics, consumes the energy, time, wealth and lives of those who play at it. It is an all-or-nothing, life-and-death conflict that is the very opposite of freedom. The game is played at various levels: the economic; the diplomatic (including deception, double-dealing, double-crossing and barefaced mendacity); treaty-making and treaty-breaking; competitive armament in which each sovereign nation or military bloc tries to outpoint rivals in mobile fire-power, and finally in local, limited, general and total wars, fought latterly with total weapons. The basic purpose of military combat is to establish a superiority in coercive agencies that will compel the enemy to surrender. At every stage in this conflict pattern principle is sacrificed to expediency and freedom to compulsion and coercion.

Defeated peoples have their countries occupied by the armed forces of the victor nations. They are reduced to vassalage and are exploited. Colonies and subject peoples rebel, usually in the name of freedom, fight their way to independence, establish themselves as sovereign states and pass through the costly grind of survival struggles. Victors enjoy brief periods of local or general supremacy, built upon coercive power, until their rivals and victims can establish a coalition sufficiently strong to topple the master nation from its position of supremacy, upset the power balance, and open the way for the next round of competitive struggle.

Anyone who questions the correctness of this analysis should read Cunningham's *Western Civilization* or any other general history of Europe during the past five or six centuries, or follow the history of Spain, Holland, France or Great Britain during the same period. Spokesmen for the chief western powers, especially during the past century, have talked volubly about freedom, but their ultimate reliance is upon compulsion exerted through armies, navies and air forces.

Significantly, during the 19th century, the power-politics pattern was modified somewhat by repeated attempts to establish a balance of power that would reduce the chances of war and substitute negotiation for conflict. Ordinarily it was the dominant powers that sought to prolong their ascendancy through a network of alliances. Ordinarily the balance was upset by a rival alliance.

Beginning with the Hague Conference in 1899, repeated attempts were made to establish the "We" principle in international relations. From World Court to League of Nations to United Nations and through many minor international bodies efforts were made to control international procedure and practice by international law. At each stage top-dog nations refused to limit their sovereignty, and particularly their right to manufacture and stockpile lethal weapons. Although the demand for disarmament was world-wide, through decade after decade the leading nations were lavishing brains, money and productive power on the development of ever more destructive means of coercion and compulsion.

Group freedom of action at the national level has led thus far to the restraint and subjugation of the individual, to the expansion and aggrandisement of certain nations at the expense of their neighbors; to conquest and subjugation of weaker peoples and their compulsory inclusion in power complexes such as empires. Group freedom of action at the national level has led to power concentration and monopoly; to the subjugation of entire continents; to wars at all levels, from colonial rebellions to local and general wars, and finally, since 1945, to the stockpiling of atomic and nuclear weapons that threaten the human race with extermination. If this be the result of group freedom at the national level, it would seem as though the human family faced a choice between the imposition of increasing restraints upon sovereign nations or the continuation of the struggle for wealth, prestige and power, progressive armament, the line-up of nations into rival power groups, and a general international war which might make the planet Earth uninhabitable for human beings.

## 22.  FREEDOM AND RESTRAINT UNDER CORPORATE BUSINESS ENTERPRISE

Economic and political activities in power age bourgeois society have centered more and more around corporate business enterprise. Relatively small personally-conducted businesses were the rule during the early phases of capitalism, although "chartered companies" were a factor even at that stage. At first gradually, then rapidly toward the end of the 19th century, the small enterpriser was replaced by big business corporations, trusts and cartels, operating first nationally and then internationally.

Throughout its history, bourgeois society has emphasized freedom from the restraints imposed by a more or less static pattern of land monopoly, the direction of social policy by landlords, soldiers and clerics, and the compulsory attachment of the masses of humanity as slaves or serfs to primitive agriculture. As the concentration of wealth and power in the hands of business corporations progressed to its monopoly or near-monopoly phase, the business spokesmen have made "freedom" the chief slogan of their propaganda, using it to popularize the bourgeois social pattern and sell it to the industrial and agricultural masses.

During the early stages of its development, modern business was winning its claim to exist and prosper without interference by a state apparatus in which landowners, hereditary aristocrats, soldiers and clerics were the chief figures. A relatively small factor in a society whose ruling elements scorned business, trade and commerce picked their way through a maze of restrictions designed to limit business activity and subordinate it to the more legitimate interests of landlords, aristocrats and ecclesiasts. In this hostile atmosphere the forerunners of modern business made their way as individual enterprisers or as concerns dominated by a single family.

Human society tends to convert practices into institutions. As business grew and prospered despite the scorn and opposition of feudal masters, expanding enterprises sought stability and security in a form more stable and permanent than the personal life span. The answer was the chartered company or corporation, operating under a charter granted by the state and authorized to carry on specified types of activity. In political terms the shareholders were the citizens of this legally created entity. The charter was its birth certificate. Under its anonymity and limited liability a succession of individuals could hold title to the property and direct its activities. Like the church and the state, business was institutionalized and thus became one of the recognized and accepted pillars upholding the structure of modern society.

Having become a pillar of organized society, recognized by the state and authorized to carry on its activities under state auspices, the incorporated business community redirected its ideology. No longer was it seeking "liberty" from feudal restraints. That battle had been won. Now it demanded "freedom" to expand its wealth and the scope of its control—at first in its particular locality and line of activity, then over wider geographical areas and varied occupational forms. Having reached the national frontier, the business corporation took the next step, crossed the frontier, and under arrangements with foreign business corporations, established the international corporation, cartel or trust which plays such an important part in present-day economy.

In the course of this development, business corporations chartered by the state reached a point in their accumulation of wealth from which they could influence and to a greater or less degree direct state policy.

This cycle of advance by corporations which were originally chartered wards of the state to positions from which they could dominate the state, provides us with one of the most significant examples of freedom in action. First, because of the rapid increase in the volume of corporate enterprise; second, because of its spread into all fields of economic endeavor; third, because of the increase in political authority of corporations; fourth, because the business corporation has become the central factor in formulating and implementing public policy; and fifth, because this climb from the status of tolerated interloper to ownership and mastery of the economy, the state and the apparatus of public information and communication has been achieved under the successive slogans of "liberty" and "freedom."

"Freedom" was no abstraction for the world-girdling corporate business enterprises of the late 19th and early 20th centuries. In order to get their strangle-hold on economics and politics, they depended upon: (1) freedom to own, organize and administer the basic means of production, to pocket the profit and live, parasitically, on the rent, interest and dividends paid to the owners of the economy; (2) freedom to experiment, discover, invent and establish patent monopolies; (3) freedom to acquire and accumulate wealth and power for their own purposes; (4) freedom to grow, consolidate and expand nationally and internationally; (5) freedom to compete, and either unite with or destroy their rivals; (6) freedom to risk (gamble) with other people's money for their own profit; (7) freedom to expropriate and exploit through economic means (sale and purchase) or through the agency of the state (franchises, subsidies, intervention, invasion, conquest, political occupation) territories which yielded profits for business enterprises; (8) freedom to advertise and propagandize through the channels of information and communication which they owned and/or directed.

During its cycle of expansion from provincial European beginnings to the planet-wide hegemony which it achieved in the late 19th century, corporate business enterprise or "western civilization" extended its geographic area of control at the same time that it broke up old culture patterns and replaced them or modified them in the interest of and for the anticipated profit of the corporate enterprisers.

Thus the industrialization or modernization of Europe, with its accompanying colonization and Europeanization of the earth, gave the entire human family opportunity to sample and experience the contributions of corporate business enterprise. These results began at the consumer level with glass beads and printed calico and extended to hardware, tools, implements, appliances and a wide variety of novelties and gadgets. They also included various means of communication, of which the printing press, photography and the radio were among the most important. They covered the field from resource utilization to brain-washing. Chiefly the results were on the surface. They never went very deep.

Corporate business was served by science and utilized the technology developed by engineering. Using freedom for its slogan ("free enterprise"; "the free world") it multiplied, manipulated, unified, consolidated, automated, monopolized locally, nationally and to an increasing degree internationally. The goal was a nationwide and worldwide network of economic and political organization in which corporate business enterprisers and their handymen were free to accumulate wealth and concentrate power in their own hands.

At the end of a century during which business enterprise had achieved its greatest triumphs in the production of wealth and the accumulation and consolidation of power, Great Britain staged one of its most impressive pageants, the Victoria Jubilee of 1897. The theme of the Jubilee was peace, progress and prosperity, established and maintained through the eight freedoms essential to the success of the business enterprisers, whose objective was the domination and exploitation of the planet. From the five continents, and across the seven seas, representatives of British interests journeyed to London to pay their respects to Queen Victoria and with her to celebrate her long and successful reign over the United Kingdom and its Empire.

Britons boasted that the sun never set on the Victorian British realm, which included almost a quarter of the earth's land mass and a like proportion of its population. British business enterprise was manufacturing and selling goods, buying raw materials and investing money around the globe. The pound sterling was the world's monetary standard. British business, through its establishments inside and outside the British Isles, and its merchant fleet, transported, financed, insured. Through the consular and diplomatic service, backed by the army and the world-dominant British navy, London made policy and enforced it. British law and the English language were rapidly becoming world law and world language. Economically and politically the British owned or controlled all four corners at the planetary crossroads.

The Victoria Jubilee came at the end of the British Century, during which crucial economic and political decisions were made in London and applied and enforced around the world. British corporate business, the British Nation and Empire, with its lords spiritual and temporal, its civil services, diplomatic and military agencies and its elaborate network of public relations, were the virtual masters of the planet. Other empires—Assyria, Egypt, Greece, Rome, had come and gone. The British Empire had about it a quality of stability and permanency which Britons recognized and acclaimed and which non-Britons challenged at their peril.

The British Empire was "free" in the sense that Britons were in a position to make money and extend their political control as fast and as far as their resources and limitations permitted them to go. Inside the British Isles natural resources were diminishing. Outside, limitations were growing. The most restrictive of these limitations was the growth of overhead costs.

Overhead costs place restrictive limits on every phase of human activity. Perhaps they can best be illustrated from experience with food surpluses on one side of a mountain range and famine on the other side. Transportation across the mountains is limited to arduous climbing over perilous trails. A carrier starts on the journey with a full load of grain. Each day he must eat enough of his load to sustain his strength. Before he can reach the famine area he has consumed his entire load. The costs of carrying have used up the load carried.

In the pattern of western civilization, illustrated by the 19th century British Empire, expansion created a heavy burden of overhead costs such as (1) cost of communication and transportation over land and seas; (2) burocratic costs of maintaining the network of economic, political and social relationships; (3) wastes of economic rivalry and competition; (4) policing costs, armament races, wars; (5) colonial unrest, sabotage, boycott and revolt; (6) burdens of parasitism based upon unearned income for the privileged at the imperial center and in the colonies and dependencies; (7) social revolutionary ferment in the homeland; (8) the costs of concessions, reforms and fringe benefits embodied in the welfare state. There is nothing new or unusual in overhead costs. They dog the footsteps of every human enterprise by eating up labor power and materials without making any corre-

168

sponding contribution to community income. The more extensive and more complex the enterprise, the higher the overhead costs.

Western civilization has girdled the planet during recent centuries. Its slogan was first "liberty," later "freedom." It justified its activities by its own "progress" and by its "liberation" of backward peoples. After a century of "liberty," followed by a century of "freedom" for western civilization to impose its pattern on the planet, the world was a slave camp. The majority of the human race lived in colonies and dependencies operated, directed and when necessary coerced by tiny oligarchies, located chiefly in western Europe. In these centers of imperial power the great majority were wage slaves, persuaded to support the corporate jobowners and masters by judicious distributions of bread, beer and circuses. The pampered middle classes, the chief reliance of the oligarchy in its efforts to expand, rule and exploit, lived in a semi-parasitic paradise that doped, demoralized, degraded and corrupted morals, manners, world outlooks.

These procedures were enveloped in a propaganda barrage employing such words as freedom, democracy, civil liberties, the rights of man. Behind the barrage was the elaborate structure of exploitation, discrimination, segregation, the police state and the organized fire-power of the armed forces.

Examination of this modern experience with imperialism-colonialism in the context of its freedom professions leads to five inescapable conclusions:

FIRST. In the field of economics, corporate business consolidation and near-monopoly have largely replaced competition among small business enterprises. Competition is described by its advocates as the essence of economic freedom.

SECOND. Assembly line conformity and automation in production and business administration is being increasingly substituted for spontaneity, personal initiative and craftsmanship.

169

THIRD. Civil liberties, specified in constitutions, legislative acts and court decisions, are among the remnants of the freedoms proclaimed and guaranteed during the early stages in the development of bourgeois society. Even these pseudo-freedoms are restricted by public authorities in the name of "security," eroded and undermined by police-state governments and in case of war or public danger are restricted or abrogated.

FOURTH. As representative bourgeois governments reach the phase of general social crisis and become fascist, constitutional procedures are replaced by personal and often by military dictatorships, civil liberties are abolished and pronouncements concerning freedom and equal justice under law yield place to denial of the simpler freedoms, to discrimination and the suppression of opposition.

FIFTH. Military preparations, competition in armaments, cold war and hot war, inflation and expropriation (the last words in compulsion and coercion), became accepted bourgeois practices

Step by step, often in the name of freedom, bourgeois society in the final phases of its decline and disintegration has promulgated decrees and adopted measures that repudiate the foundation principles enunciated by the business interests during their struggle to replace their feudal predecessors and establish bourgeois hegemony over the planet. Of all the big lies peddled to an ignorant, credulous public during the past two centuries, the freedom lie is probably the biggest and the most bare-faced.

Under corporate business enterprise, at the imperial centers of wealth and power, social crisis leads away from the practice of freedom toward its denial. Among the colonial and dependent peoples economic, political and racial subordination and discrimination were taken for granted during the heyday of corporate business control. At the turn of the century a billion human beings inhabiting the colonies and dependencies of corporate business controlled empires were regarded and treated as second-rate citizens in their own homelands, which had been conquered, occupied by the armed might of governments under corporate business control, and exploited economically by the emissaries of profit-seeking corporate business enterprise.

These steps away from freedom and toward restraint and coercion are neither accidental nor incidental. Rather, they are implicit in the competitive struggle for wealth and power which constitutes the central ideological and practical purpose of bourgeois society.

Three roads are available to mankind in the general social crisis which has arisen because of the exercise, by corporate business enterprise, of the eight freedoms listed on a previous page of this chapter.

ROAD I: Return to the social pattern as it existed before the War of 1914-18, the Mexican Revolution of 1910, the Chinese Revolution of 1911 and the Russian Revolution of 1917. The pattern will be modified by the transformation through which western civilization is passing, within the restrictions imposed by historical developments. It will be a restoration of the social outlooks and practices prevalent in West Europe and the United States at the turn of the century. Such a choice appeals to those individuals and communities that resent change and cling to the past because it is familiar and comfortable. The clock of history can be turned back temporarily, as Spain, South Korea and Taiwan bear witness, but the process involves not freedom but ruthless coercion.

ROAD II: Liberalize and humanize the 19th century pattern of exploitation, discrimination and segregation based on imperialism-colonialism, leaving intact the principles of competition, individual acquisition and accumulation of private property, private enterprise, economic expansion and national sovereignty, but with the ameliorative features of the welfare state, provided primarily for the peoples of the imperial homelands, but in modified form for peoples of colonies and dependencies. Such courses of action are being followed in the homelands of all of the 19th century empires, their associates and dependencies. Under these "liberalized" conditions freedoms would be watered down, modified and controlled.

ROAD III: Reconstruct the social order on the principles of cooperation, coordination, social ownership and administration of the social means of production, the distribution of income in accordance with need and the subordination of national sovereignty to the overall interests of the human family under the direction of a competent world authority, thus applying to human affairs, at the world level, the same rational judgments that individual humans are expected to apply to their own personal affairs. This course of action implies the use of science and technology by the community, to advance community interests and subordinate freedom to the general welfare. It also means remodeling or scrapping the principles and essential practices of 19th century western civilization. Efforts to establish the program in the socialist countries are being fought stubbornly by every agency at the disposal of corporate business enterprise.

No matter which of these three roads 20th century man decides to follow, the going will be rough at least temporarily. The urgencies and imperatives of the crisis precipitated by the exercise of the several freedoms of western civilization can be met only by fateful decisions and heroic actions that will subordinate freedom and maximise restraint for the period of the emergency. No other perspective is rationally thinkable in a period of drastic social transformation such as that through which bourgeois society is presently passing.

## 23. FREEDOM, RESTRAINT AND SOCIAL TRANSITION

Under conditions of power age economic and political inter-dependence, group survival and the advancement of group inter-ests must take precedence over the survival and advancement of any of the individuals who make up the group. This conclusion is based upon an examination of the structure and function of power age communities. In a power age society the contributions toward survival and success made by the group are more signifi-cant than parallel contributions made by individuals. The title role in the power age is played by "We-ness." At best "I-ness" has a minor place in the drama.

Another aspect of the problem requires consideration. Power age society in the mid-20th century is neither static nor stable. On the contrary, the introduction of power age techniques has developed a social fluidity that has led to rapid and basic changes in social structure and function. Inauguration of power age tech-nology renders pre-power age techniques more or less obsolete and replaces them with a new social outlook and a drastically altered social apparatus. Parts of the West have been passing through this radical transition since the early stages of the indus-trial revolution. Changes in the field of science and technology have been followed, in one Western country after another, by modifications in political and social institutions and practices. Other parts of the planet are also undergoing parallel experiences.

Periods of social transition and transformation necessarily are periods of imbalance and instability. Whatever the causative factors behind the transition, the changes in themselves disturb the status and alter the outlook of various social groups, generating individual feelings of uncertainty and anxiety.

The more deep-running and far-reaching the social transformation, the greater will be its upsetting effect on the social and psychological balance of the community. Minor political disturbances occasioned by general elections or by shifts in political administration may pass almost unnoticed. But disturbances arising from changes in technology, which lead to production in excess of market demand, create unemployment, and force up the cost of living, cannot fail to upset individual and group life.

Where social transition is accompanied by domestic revolution and counter-revolution, or where it involves foreign intervention, the resulting unbalance will probably lead to civil war. Events in Spain after 1931 provide an excellent example of a situation involving industrialization in a semi-feudal community, a political shift following an election, the abolition of the monarchy, the inauguration of a republic, the adoption of a constitution which proposed to liberalize the political apparatus, extend social security, conserve and develop natural resources, and separate an established church from the state. A military coup led by army officers and aided by foreign intervention (ideological, political and military) and devastating civil war (1936-39) was won by the conservative and reactionary elements with extensive aid from abroad. Similar transitions have taken place on every continent during the shift from a pre-industrial to a power age economy. The movement began in Europe, was extended to the Americas and more recently reached Asia and Africa, where one people after another shook off the yoke of foreign control and moved toward independence and self-determination.

Chapter 19 of this book dealt with The Relativity of Freedom. This relativeness involves constant modifications in the freedom-restraint balance since alterations in the direction and intensity of social forces have their counterpart first in the social life pattern and ultimately in that of individuals, families and local groups.

Periods of social transition, with consequent disturbance and disruption in economic, political and social affairs, push the line of public policy away from freedom and toward restraint. Any major social emergency, no matter what its cause, leads to a shift in the freedom-restraint balance. The greater the revolutionary or counter-revolutionary thrust from within, and the more extensive the intervention and invasion from without, the greater will be the restraints imposed in order to preserve the social equilibrium.

Another factor which complicates social transformation is the matter of time. With a basic economic development such as change in technology, the time element is subordinate. Such changes run their long-term course, providing both a potent upsetting force and a background against which other changes take place.

Emergencies caused by transfers of political power from person to person or group to group, or emergencies occasioned by intervention or invasion from outside the local community, may be brief and incidental and therefore have little permanent effect upon the transition process. Or they may take a more permanent form such as the conquest and occupation of Finland by Russia after 1808, or the setting up of the Franco dictatorship in Spain after 1939. To call such developments emergencies may do an injustice to the ordinary use of the word. But the old social pattern is definitely and sharply altered, and the local population is called upon to adapt itself to an essentially new situation. In all such adaptations, if the social forces are skillfully handled by the policy makers, farmers and craftsmen may step from one social pattern into another without too much difficulty. The same thing may be true of coddled and properly conditioned white collar elements in the population. Industrial workers may grumble a bit but will go along with the new order, if supplied with bread, beer and circuses. Under severe economic or political pressures, however, industrial workers, if thoroughly organized, may be counted on to resist and rebel. Always under such circumstances professional and intellectual elements will prove a serious stumbling block. With sufficient economic means and skill, they can be quieted temporarily. Almost inevitably the intellectuals will build up resistance and often will lead revolt.

Through such emergencies concessions made at an opportune moment and properly advertised and popularised will help hold disaffection to a minimum. In the background, however, will be the police and the military, trained and equipped to employ sufficient coercion and compulsion to maintain social stability.

Such a situation, with the old order losing its influence and grip and passing from the scene, and the new order not yet established, involves an uneasy social balance. Under these conditions a quick thrust from one side or the other may shift the power balance, as it did in Russia between 1916 and 1920. In the face of such uncertainties and emergencies, freedoms will probably be decreased, at least temporarily, and the course of public policy be shifted far toward the restraint pole of the freedom-restraint equilibrium.

If the new social pattern is relatively permanent, the oncoming generation, through indoctrination, compulsory schooling and economic and military conscription, may adjust and accustom itself to the situation in which it was born and has grown up.

Patterns will be modified by the conditions existing in different countries, but in the early stages of social emergency, restraint and the threat of restraint will play a dominant role which under competent leadership may be gradually modified as the population becomes accustomed and therefore reconciled to the changed situation. Such adjustments take time however, during which freedom is minimized, and restraint even though successfully camouflaged is always ready at hand, like a fire-fighting company, prepared for instant action when the alarm sounds.

As the transition matures, power age peoples reach a level of social organization, control and administration that promises an era of stability and security. As each community approaches its new social equilibrium, public policy veers away from restraint toward freedom.

The rapidity with which policy makers shift away from restraint toward freedom depends upon six factors: (1) the completion of the transformation from competitive power struggle for personal and local advantage to the public use of power for the advancement of the general welfare; (2) general understanding of the course of events and consequent mass support for the new social evironment; (3) experience, social maturity and social awareness of those in authority; (4) the intensity of the competitive struggle for power which led up to the new level of understanding and stability and the extent to which, in the community, antagonism, hatred and bitterness have carried over from the previous era of instability and insecurity; (5) the willingness of the formerly dominant elements to recognize defeat, accept subordination and team up in an all-out effort to gain maximum advantage on the new level of social equilibrium from the new era of expanding freedom; (6) success of the new order in providing first an improvement in the necessaries of life, and later, the conveniences and amenities.

Where transition and transformation are achieved without

counter-revolution, an early swing away from restraint toward freedom may be expected. If the forces of counter-revolution are strategically placed, well led, abundantly financed and strongly supported by an energetic middle class and a well-organized oligarchy which includes dominant elements from farm and labor organizations, attention may be centered and energies may be consumed for long periods in the struggle between the supporters of the new order and the counter-revolutionary forces, opposing change and proposing a return to the old social pattern. Such a stalemate may postpone the establishment of a particular community on the new level of power age security and stability.

If those responsible for policy making during the transition period are greedy, selfish and short-sighted; if they bungle, blunder, personalize or tyrannize, or if they invoke foreign aid in an effort to extricate themselves from tangled domestic situations, tensions will be heightened, civil strife will be aggravated and prolonged, and the course of public policy will continue on the restraint side of the freedom-restraint arc.

Transition to the power age, with its advanced science and technology, if directed with maximum intelligence, imagination and competence, may entail minimum losses and result in maximum gains. Under such conditions the social costs of the transition may be kept low. With limited experience and incompetence in direction and control, the social costs may become excessive and may open the door to disaffection and ultimately to counter-revolution.

First steps are the most difficult in any enterprise. In the case of industrialization and under social planning the first steps have been taken, the experiences have been evaluated and the danger points noted and marked. In the light of accumulating experience, subsequent transitions to power age economies should be made at low cost and with little disruption of the social equilibrium.

Each individual, each neighborhood, each locality, each community must emancipate itself from pre-power age limitations and must equip itself to function effectively and cooperatively on the power age level. It is not enough to read or talk about the transition from the old society to the new. All who propose to live as effective, useful elements in power age society must be re-educated and re-oriented for power age citizenship and participation in power age group life.

## 24. FREEDOM, RESTRAINT AND SOCIALIST CONSTRUCTION

Power age culture is dominated in its early phases by three imperative historical factors: (1) the rapid tempo at which discovery and invention, operating through science and technology, have brought the power age into being; (2) the disturbing, upsetting and uprooting consequences of dismantling an established social pattern in one generation, and (3) substituting for a long-established culture pattern a new pattern better adapted to power age realities and more adequate to withstand the buffeting of forced-draft social transition. During a revolutionary period of headlong transition and far-reaching social transformation (at least in its present early stages) the course of social development shifts away from freedom toward restraint and away from minor local restraints and directives toward major and general restraints and directives.

Part of the reason for this shift away from freedom toward restraint is the instability and uncertainty that are unavoidable accompaniments of any sharp change in direction. Another part lies in the necessity of learning and at the same time teaching a new way of life. During the crucial transition period entire communities cease to follow their accustomed procedures, and work out new ones with all of the attending shifts in individual and social attitudes, outlooks and action patterns.

The three above-mentioned forces have played an important role in communities that have developed corporative or welfare states. They have been even more in evidence among peoples who have attempted to build socialism.

Corporatism and welfarism are new in detail but not in principle. Communities that have developed these social forms have been able to preserve much of the theory and practice of the old society. This is notably true in Europe with its comparatively long feudal past and its extended experience with capitalism. In Britain's corporative state, as in Sweden's welfare state, private enterprise and private ownership of the means of production, monarchy and an established, official church all persist as recognized pillars of a dominantly acquisitive society. Scientific and technical advances have been initiated and promoted in these and other communities that have played a prominent role in working out the new culture patterns that ushered in the power age.

Socialist construction, on the other hand, involved not merely changes in the detail of social organization and direction, but the conception and formulation of new principles, the renovation and adaptation of old ones and their utilization in novel practices and greatly modified institutions in areas that were largely rural, pre-industrial, illiterate, and unacquainted with the experimental or laboratory attitude toward life and its problems. This description applies to the Soviet Union in 1917, to Eastern Europe (with minor exceptions) in 1945, to India and Ceylon in 1947 and to China in 1949. Indeed, the description, with a few notable exceptions, applied to the entire world of colonies and dependencies from which the industrialized and modernized areas of the planet drew cheap raw materials and cheap labor, and in which they marketed a large share of their exported goods and services.

Europeanization of the planet during the four centuries that followed the voyaging and discovering of the 15th century maintained a well-established pattern of expansion and more or less compulsory acculturation. With exploration went the essentials of European culture. Traders followed explorers, offering the natives European products in exchange for native goods and services. Then came land seizure, capital investment in living quarters, warehouses and port facilities, occupation by units of the army and navy, settlement by immigrants, deals with the local elite and, where these deals proved difficult, armed invasion and occupation. Local elites frequently staged revolts against foreign intervention and attempted to establish independent and self-determining cultures of their own, modeled more or less after the culture pattern of the occupying power. The United States, from discovery and colonization through revolt, independence and self-determination, is a good example of the process. These changes involved readjustments, growing pains, revolt and war, but the central purpose was the continuation of the old culture pattern in a new geographical location.

At no point in the transformation of Europe from a feudal to a bourgeois social pattern and the construction of bourgeois culture centers in the Americas and Australasia did corporative or welfare communities escape from drastic restraints and

181

coercions. As we have seen, the so-called "free world" has more than its share of restrictions and compulsions as exemplified in the bourgeois state apparatus, in the remnants of exploitive, profit-dominated economies, in the concept of master races and the innate superiority of European culture patterns to "native" patterns existing elsewhere. The widely advertised civil rights and liberties of the West did not emerge, fully formulated from the English, American and French revolutions. Rather they developed gradually through centuries of experiment and struggle. Chattel slavery was a legal institution in the United States until 1863. Racial discrimination and segregation persist today in many Western countries. In Britain, the cradle of bourgeois democracy, full adult suffrage was secured, after btiter struggles, only during the present century. Hereditary monarchy and aristocracy, imperialism-colonialism and job-ownership by the privileged few persist down to the present day. Seven centuries passed after the signing of Magna Carta in 1215 A.D. before the present corporative society with its feudal remnants and welfare trimmings was achieved in the British Isles.

Compared with the century long efforts of western man to establish, carry on and improve the theory and practice of bourgeois life, socialism has hardly emerged from the womb of history. Socialist theories date back for about two centuries. Aside from primitive communal living and the organization of special small communities, the actual advent of socialism in practice came with the Mexican, Chinese and Russian revolutions of 1910, 1911 and 1917.

Thus far in a stormy and checkered career attempts to build socialism in mature bourgeois communities have broken down or have been suppressed by the bourgeois government immediately involved or by political and military intervention and invasion from neighboring bourgeois states. Only in the back country of pre-industrial economy and colonial disaffection have attempts to build socialism achieved even the beginnings of success.

Socialist construction in agrarian, pre-industrial, pre-scientific, illiterate, superstition-bound communities began with the changes that converted semi-feudal, partially industrialized dependencies and colonies of the world empires into independent bourgeois states. It moved beyond that point, into social ownership of land and other socially productive forces, social and economic planning and the subordination of the competitive wealth-power struggle, to a cooperative effort to establish social justice and equalize opportunity. Such a revolutionary approach to the general social crisis involved the development of new principles and new techniques of organization.

Instead of a program of the minor reforms embodied in corporative and welfare states which presupposed no drastic departures from the customary way of life, socialist construction violated the principles, ran counter to the practices and challenged the accepted life patterns of habit-ridden herdsmen and cultivators. Not only did the new social order contravene the old, but it required a population accustomed to time-honored rule-of thumb procedures, to study and learn new and alien theories and techniques. It demanded that illiterate peoples turn from accustomed individual and social routine, learn to read and write, delve into science, acquire painstaking techniques, experiment in chemistry, physics, biology, soil science, hydraulics and electronics, engage in mass construction projects based on general long-term plans, with specific and local short-term plans designed to build a pattern of society which had existed heretofore only in the minds of utopian theorists. Such a program, in its larger aspects, meant not merely the rationalization of traditional and customary social patterns, but large-scale efforts to master, modify and utilize nature.

Such a task was not merely gigantic; it took on the qualities of magic. When Lenin proposed, in 1920, to have electricity in every city, village and farm home of Russia by 1970, a span of fifty years, the idea sounded preposterous. Had it been enunciated by the priest in the name of religion, it would have seemed heretical, but it was propounded and promoted in the name of an unknown and almost unheard-of good—socialism—which all true believers had been taught to regard as godless and intrinsically evil.

Blazing this path across unknown country, through and around unanticipated obstacles toward an untried future, smacked of madness, especially when the task had to be undertaken and carried to a successful, experimental conclusion by families and villages of largely illiterate farmers, herdsmen, wood-cutters, hunters and fishermen, most of whom asked nothing better than to be let alone to follow their traditional way of life. Had they been uncoerced, this is the line of action that these custom- and habit-bound peoples would certainly have followed. They were prevented from doing so by three coercive forces: the disrupting pressures generated by developing science and technology, the destructivity of all-out war, and the promise of a pot of gold and a good life at the end of the socialist rainbow.

Once they had set out on their perilous journey into the promised land, other forces compelled them to go on: the momentum of a mass purpose to survival and betterment, efforts of the counter-revolution to drive them back, and the leadership of a dedicated minority which accepted and believed in the iron discipline of communism.

There was another lure. For the imaginative and venturesome the proposed new life offered a vision of experiment and endeavor in which literally millions would have a vital part in taming nature and organizing society. In a word they would demolish the cultural shacks and hovels in which most members of the human race had been living and replace them by mansions worthy of reason, beauty and social justice.

Such a statesmanlike project would cover six inter-related fields. (1) The utilization and conservation of the great variety and unmeasured abundance of nature's resources, with heretofore unknown and unused sources of energy heading the list. (2) Understanding and utilizing to the full human creative genius to design, build and employ implements, tools, machines and formulas needed, on one hand, to deal with nature forces and materials, and on the other hand to produce the goods and services necessary to develop and operate a complicated productive and social apparatus. The going in such an endeavor is bound to be rough because the limitations imposed by ignorance, custom and habit work hand in hand with vested interests rooted in the old social order. In the early stages of building a mechanized, planned, publicly owned and managed economy, many would have to wait and perhaps tighten their belts, while they made the machines that would produce the implements that eventually would provide economic abundance. (3) Building a political apparatus that would be responsible for the smooth-functioning of the new economy, that would have as its object the greatest good to the greatest number and the least harm to the smallest number, and that would be accessible at all times to the people on one side and the various national and cultural segments composing the population on the other. (4) Subsidizing science, promoting education, encouraging and supporting the arts. (5) Maintaining the interest of the younger generation, enlisting its support, evoking its enthusiasm, harnessing its energies to the common purpose, and securing its participation in the task of building up and improving the new social order. (6) Sharing opportunity, leisure, advancement and higher standards of well-being with ever-widening circles of the population.

Spokesmen for the West frequently compare West and East in terms of the variety and extent of the freedoms available under capitalism and socialism. Such comparisons are misleading, first, because the socialist sector of the world is in a very early stage of its development, while the capitalist sector has rounded out centuries of experiment and experience. The second reason is of a far more fundamental nature. The free enterprise capitalist sector has emphasized freedom from its early beginnings, when businessmen were hampered by feudal restrictions and obstructions. In capitalist society each citizen is free to make money and to spend such portions of it as the government does not take in direct and indirect taxes. Capitalism is built around a purchase and sale, or price and money relationship. It is from price and money transactions, based on private ownership of land and productive instruments, and from the sale and purchase of labor power that capitalists reap their profits. Socialists look upon all such relationships as exploitive and anti-social. Capitalists want to acquire and accumulate personal fortunes. Socialists and communists want to work together on projects that will raise the standard of well-being by promoting the common weal or general welfare.

Capitalists demand freedom to advance their individual interests. Socialists are looking for means of promoting the interests of the community,—the general interests.

From the essential nature of capitalism and socialism arises a third reason that makes freedom an invalid basis of comparison between the two social systems. Capitalists want freedom to compete in the struggle for wealth and power. The highest form of competition is war. Throughout the entire course of Western civilization rival capitalists have waged cold wars and hot wars

186

against each other. Recent experience has led to the inescapable conclusion that total war fought with presently available weapons will result in total destruction. Thus, freedom to compete means freedom to commit collective suicide.

Socialists, on the other hand, emphasise cooperation—an emphasis on the "We" aspects of human life. They argue that both survival and improvement are possible only in terms of common or collective endeavor. The test of the workability of any social system is its capacity to survive and to improve. The significant basis for judging the worth of a social order is not the freedom it provides, but its capacity to survive and to improve. Therefore it is in terms of survival and improvement that a social system should be judged and a comparison between different social systems should be made.

Socialist construction aims to conserve and improve the natural and social environments, broaden opportunity, adapt to emerging situations and bring the benefits of group activity to larger elements of the population. Goals like abundance, security, justice and improvement must be clearly stated, explained, understood, agreed upon. Moving step by step toward a goal requires a workable plan and time-table that can be adjusted to the wide variation of conditions existing on the planet; a trained and trusted leadership dedicated to promote the general welfare, maintaining and broadening mass support; a mass following and a carefully trained corps of apprentices qualified and equipped to take over and carry on.

Such a program for establishing and maintaining a workable human society on this planet must give first priority to the task of building, perpetuating and improving the new social structure. Freedom is not its immediate goal. At the same time it must provide a range of freedom consistent with the purposes, construction and the operation of the new society.

## 25. FREEDOM AND RESPONSIBILITY IN THE POWER AGE

Advances in knowledge and in its application to the daily processes of individual and group living have greatly increased man's capacity to utilize and control both the natural and the social environment. Every advance in power to control carries with it more than a corresponding increase in responsibility for the consequences of disturbing the pre-established equilibrium between nature, society and humanity.

Specifically, man who only a few years ago walked across level land at four miles an hour, ran for short distances at fifteen or twenty miles, and dashed on horseback at twenty-five or thirty miles, now moves by automobile at sixty or eighty miles, by jet plane at more than five hundred miles an hour and by space ship at more than twenty thousand miles an hour. Increased speeds carry with them greatly augmented responsibilities,—for safety, for accelerated consumption of energies and raw materials. More important, shrinking time and distance bring men closer together in one world with the drastic choice of coexistence or conflict, ending possibly in annihilation.

Having called down "fire-from-heaven" (the power of the split atom), mankind has assumed responsibility for the use of the resultant energy. Once man has released such forces they do not remain inert, but are radioactive,—in a state of constant and at times explosive change. Nature's forces may be employed constructively to probe farther into the mysteries and release still more potent thunderbolts or else they may be used to tear down and rubbleize the entire structure of human culture.

Increased control over nature and society may inflate egos and whet power-hunger, or it may augment self-consciousness and self-confidence, develop social awareness and lead to greater at-one-ness of the self conscious and socially conscious individual with the total life of the community and the cosmos. Each of these steps—self consciousness, social consciousness and cosmic consciousness, carries with it an added share of responsibility for the total well-being of the individual, the community and the universe.

Responsibility dogs man's footsteps. The farther he goes and the faster he moves, the more complications and problems he encounters. On the other hand, as man moves faster and farther, new vistas and enlarged opportunities open before him.

Power age man faces possibilities for a quick and decisive advance, perhaps a big leap; physically, in his control over the earth and its resources; sociologically, in establishing a planned, remodeled, just, rational, harmonious, beautiful, planet-wide society; cosmically, in his penetration and investigation of the island universe of which earth is a part; psychologically, in his understanding and re-direction of himself and his creative potentialities.

Whether man advances, using his enlarged knowledge and experience to take his place among the builders and creators, or drifts and slips into another dark age of hit-or-miss recuperation, stock-taking and social reorganization, or rushes frantically into an orgy of destruction that will end in annihilation, the extension or restriction of freedom will remain a sensitive problem area. Imaginative, creative, constructive, inventive individuals will formulate proposals, draw up plans and initiate movements to take advantage of power age opportunities, advance knowledge,

189

develop new techniques, broaden culture, improve the natural and the social environment, promote order, peace, and general well-being. Persons holding established privileged positions will resist change, increase the supply of bread, beer and circuses, appeal to tradition, custom, prejudice, fear and do their best to hold the line against innovators. Backward, custom-bound, contented elements in the populations will beg to be let alone in the enjoyment of the fleshpots which the power age has brought them. Restive, misfit intellectuals will dissent, experiment, talk, demonstrate. Ambitions, aggressive adventurers, free-booters, power-seekers, predators and plunderers will persist in gambling with their own lives and those of their contemporaries. All of these decisive factors in public life will unite in a demand for freedom in one of its many meanings. For the most dangerous elements of the population, the power-seekers, free-booters, predators and plunderers, freedom will mean self-seeking in the narrowest sense, coupled with the absence of responsibility for the sequence of events set in motion by their irresponsible adventuring.

Hence the importance of accuracy in expression and usage in any discussion of freedom, its promise and its menace. Multiple-meaning words are not merely clumsy, they are misleading to the point of acute danger. Two general wars, begun in 1914 and 1939, and dozens of local wars launched during the same period were fought in the name of freedom. The freedom cult is more voluble and vociferous today than it has been at any time in the past half-century and more dangerous to the general welfare.

Freedom as idea and freedom in action are generally useful and advantageous. At times they are of paramount importance. There are present-day circumstances under which freedom is of primary concern. But these times and circumstances are not universal in industrial society. Freedom, whether for the individual or for any social group (including the nation), is not necessarily advantageous. Before any project or program involving freedom can be given the green light, the questions should be asked: freedom for which individual or group to do what? When? Where? Employing what means? In pursuit of what purpose? In other words, there can be no unqualified or blanket endorsement of freedom.

Power age man must ask himself several searching questions about the relative importance of freedom, of opportunity and responsibility, in much the same sense that a child, growing toward man's estate, must discover and understand himself, his possibilities, and the conditions under which he is living. In infancy while movement was strictly limited, responsibility was virtually nil. At the child level, movement (in the sense of freedom to move) became one of the most significant and treasured aspects of life, without any corresponding increase in responsibilities. Then, approaching adulthood, responsibilities increased without any corresponding increase in freedoms. "But must I surrender the freedoms of my childhood for this prison house of adult responsibilities?" the harrassed individual demands. "Better remain a child than to endure such limitations." Retarded individuals frequently do exactly that—retaining the joys of childhood's relative freedom in order that they may avoid the responsibilities and burdens of adulthood.

Similarly, today, the human race is passing from a stage of lesser to a stage of greater responsibility. If human beings wish to avoid the penalties of retardation and enjoy the advantages and opportunities of adult life, they must shoulder the adult burdens of the power age, which include discipline, restrictions and control.

Perhaps it would be well to remind ourselves of the relation between freedom, duty and responsibility. For this purpose individual freedom may be defined as the right to choose, decide and act, which is the prerogative of an individual in his dealings with the group of which he is a member. Duties are the obligations which the group imposes upon its members, and which members assume and carry out under group direction. Responsibilities are the obligations which members of a group assume and carry out as their contribution to the group and its welfare. Freedoms advantage the individual, sometimes at the expense of the group. Duties, the outcome of group needs and requirements, are imposed upon individuals in order to promote the general welfare, for the advantage of the group. Responsibilities are assumed and carried by individuals and sub-groups as their contribution to the general welfare.

Variation, differentiation, deviation, opposition, competition and conflict are among the unavoidable connotations and consequences of freedom. These factors and forces may be minimized or maximized, but they are inescapable and cannot be ignored. Wherever two or three human beings are gathered together, sooner or later the freedom-restraint issue presents itself. It is the old story of the pushing insistent "I" and the urgent persistent "We,"—competition versus cooperation, or competition partially synchronized with cooperation and perhaps with compulsion and coercion.

Confronted by these fateful alternatives, predicaments and dilemmas, human beings would be wise (1) to cease idealizing, idolizing and deifying freedom; (2) to give freedom a considered rating as one of many significant human values; (3) to alter the rating of freedom with changing situations; (4) to maintain the difficult and always precarious balance between freedom at one pole and restraint (conformity, obligation, responsibility and coercion) at the other pole.

From local social groups to the world community, survival and the maintenance of order, peace and justice are possible only on the basis of an equilibrium between interests of the "I" and the requirements of the "We," between the part and the whole, between local sovereignty and world responsibility.

Man seeks to enlarge the area in which he may choose, decide and act as a result of individual effort and through group (political) guarantees, arrangements, adjustments. In each generation he contends with nature, with society, with himself—to hold what his forebears gained and to enlarge the areas of his thinking and acting. In one period the advocates of greater freedom make gains. At the next shift in the relations of social forces these gains are eroded by tyranny or swept away by power-seizure, civil strife, war, revolution. At each stage the course of social advance shifts, now toward freedom, again toward restraint.

In the population-wealth-power concentrations which bulk so large in the present age, increasing numbers of individuals cry "freedom" at every crossroads. The western world pays lip service to freedom, but is under countless pressures of multiple plans, directives, controls, regulations and restraints aimed either at the increase of wealth and power in the hands of the few or aimed at security, stability and the extension of the general welfare. In any case, the urgent human need is not greater freedom, but a crusade led by a dedicated minority to perform tasks that demand knowledge, training, experience and disciplined group action.

Freedom is not enough. The power age is in desperate need not so much of free men and women as of disciplined, responsible, dedicated citizens. Its future, nay, its very survival requires not free nations but nations and peoples willing and able to subordinate fatherland defense to the requirements of peace, justice and the common welfare. A planet-wide organization capable of assuring equal opportunity under law in a world community founded on shared abundance offers mankind the most reasonable and least costly way out of the existing crisis.

# NOTES

## NOTES TO PART I

1. N.Y.: Columbia University Press 1947 p. 3.
2. In *Freedom in the Modern World*, H. M. Kallen, Ed., N.Y.: Coward McCann 1928 p. 25.
3. In *Encyclopedia of the Social Sciences* under "Liberty."
4. *Freedom in the Modern World*, op. cit., p. 272.
5. *Freedom and History*, N.Y.: Noonday Press 1952, p. 87.
6. *Liberty and Restraint*, N.Y.: Knopf 1926, p. ix.
7. In *Freedom in the Modern World*, op. cit., p. 95.
8. Garden City, N.Y.: Doubleday 1958.
9. *Op. cit.*, pp. 11-13.
10. *Freedom in the Modern World*, op. cit., pp. 2-3.
11. Ruth N. Anshan, *Freedom, Its Meaning*, N.Y.: Harcourt Brace 1940, p. 6.
12. Ithaca, N.Y.: Cornell University Press 1943.
13. N.Y.: Monthly Review Press, 1957.
14. N.Y.: Putnam 1939, p. 8.
15. John F. Acton, *The History of Freedom*, Boston: Beacon Press 1948, p. 30.
16. *Liberty in the Modern State*, London: Faber & Faber 1930.
17. *Issues of Freedom*, N.Y.: Harpers 1959.
18. N.Y.: Harper 1960.

## NOTES TO PART II

1. N.Y.: Columbia University Press 1941 p. 37.
2. *Man's Search for the Good Life*, Harborside, Maine: Social Science Institute 1954, Chapter Two.
3. In Monroe Berger, *Freedom and Control in Modern Society*, N.Y.: Van Nostrand 1954 pp. 5-6.
4. *The Liberal Tradition in America*, N.Y.: Harcourt 1955 p. 57.

5. *Op. cit.*, p. 35.
6. *The Liberal Mind*, Ithaca, N.Y.: Cornell University Press 1948 p. 23.
7. *Freedom*, N.Y.: Stokes 1918 p. 1.
8. *Lectures on the Philosophy of History*, London: 1861 p. 476.
9. *Ibid.*, p. 18.
10. W. H. Hamilton, Freedom and Economic Necessity, in H. M. Kallen, *Freedom in the Modern World, op. cit.*, p. 49.
11. R. Baizel, *Souveranitat und Freiheit*, Koln: Baldwin Rex Verlag 1950 p. 81.
12. *Liberty in the Modern State, op. cit.*, p. 256.
13. *The Wealth of Nations*, published in 1776.
14. N.Y.: Farrar & Rinehart 1941.
15. U.S. Congressional Record, Feb. 18, 1955.
16. See *U.S.A. Today*, by Helen and Scott Nearing, Harborside, Maine: Social Science Institute 1955.

## NOTES TO PART III

1. *Op. cit.*
2. Richard McKeon, *Freedom and History, op. cit.*, p. 44, quoted from Hegel, Lectures on the Philosophy of History, London 1861, Part IV, Sect. 3, Ch. III p. 476.
3. Silas Bent, Freedom of Speech, in H. M. Kallen, *Freedom in the Modern World, op. cit.*, p. 144.
4. Philosophies of Freedom, in H. M. Kallen, *Freedom in the Modern World, op. cit.*, pp. 266-7 & 270.
5. *Liberty in the Modern State, op. cit.*, pp. 73-5.
6. *The Liberal Mind, op. cit.*, 2.27.
7. A. N. Whitehead, Aspects of Freedom, in Ruth N. Anshan, Ed., *Freedom, Its Meaning, op. cit.*, p. 62.
8. *Freedom in the Modern World, op. cit.*, p. 275.
9. On "Liberty," in *Encyclopedia of the Social Sciences*, p. 45.
10. Bound with *Social Statics*, N.Y.: Appleton 1896.
11. *Liberty in the Modern State, op. cit.*, p. 29.
12. N.Y.: Knopf 1945 p. 3.
13. *Freedom in the Modern World, op. cit.*, p. 11.

## NOTES TO PART IV

1. *Freedom, Loyalty, Dissent*, N.Y.: Oxford University Press 1954 pp. vii-viii.
2. Erich Fromm, *Escape from Freedom, op. cit.*, pp. 255-6.
3. Peter Morris, "Accessory After the Fact," in MacKenzie, Norman, Ed. *Conviction*, N.Y.: Monthly Review Press 1959 p. 179.
4. *On Being Human*, N.Y.: Shuman 1950 p. 73.

195

# BIBLIOGRAPHY

Acton, John E. *Essays on Freedom and Power.* Boston: Beacon Press 1948
Adler, Mortimer J. *The Idea of Freedom.* Garden City, N.Y.: Doubleday 1958
Anshen, Ruth N., Ed. *Freedom, Its Meaning.* N.Y.: Harcourt Brace 1940
Ascoli, Max. *The Power of Freedom.* N.Y.: Farrar, Straus 1949
Barth, Alan. *The Loyalty of Free Men.* N.Y.: Viking 1951
Barzel, Rainer. *Souveränität und Freiheit.* Köln: Pick 1950
Becker, Carl L. *Freedom and Responsibility in the American Way of Life.* N.Y.: Knopf 1945
Bennett, William. *Freedom and Liberty.* London: Oxford Univ. Press 1920
Berger, Morroe. *Freedom and Control in Modern Society.* N.Y.: Nostrand 1954
Bernal, John D. *The Freedom of Necessity.* London: Routledge & Kegan Paul 1949
Bernanos, Georges. *Plea for Liberty.* N.Y.: Pantheon 1944
Bertauld, M. A. *La Liberté Civile.* Paris: Didier 1864
Biddle, Francis. *The Fear of Freedom.* Garden City, N.Y.: Doubleday 1951
Blanshard, Paul. *The Right to Read.* Boston: Beacon Press 1955
Bryson, Lyman. *Science and Freedom.* N.Y.: Columbia Univ. Press 1947
Burckhardt, Jacob. *Force and Freedom.* N.Y.:Pantheon 1943
Burgess, John William. *The Reconciliation of Government with Liberty.* N.Y.: Scribners 1915
Bury, J. B. *History of Freedom of Thought.* N.Y.: Holt 1913
Caudwell, Christopher. *Studies in a Dying Culture.* London: John Lane 1938
Chafee, Zechariah. *The Blessings of Liberty.* Philadelphia: Lippincott 1956
Cheyney, Edward P., Ed. *Freedom of Inquiry and Expression.* Annals of the American Academy, Nov. 1938 Vol. 200
Commager, Henry Steele. *Freedom, Loyalty, Dissent.* N.Y.: Oxford Univ. Press 1935
Compton, Arthur H. *The Freedom of Man.* New Haven: Yale Univ. Press 1935
Conklin, Grant C. *Freedom and Responsibility.* Boston: Houghton Mifflin 1935
Cooper, Kent. *The Right to Know.* N.Y.: Farrar, Strauss & Cudahy 1956
Craig, Hardin. *Freedom and Renaissance.* Chapel Hill: Univ. of North Carolina Press 1949

Cranston, Maurice. *Freedom, A New Analysis*. N.Y.: Longmans Green 1953
Davis, Elmer. *But We Were Both Free*. Indianapolis: Bobbs-Merrill 1954
Dewey, John. *Freedom and Culture*. N.Y.: Putnam 1939
Douglas, William O. *An Almanac of Liberty*. Garden City, N.Y.: Doubleday 1954
Duguit, Leon. *Souveraineté et Liberté*. Paris: F. Alcan 1922
Dunham, James Henry. *Freedom and Purpose*. Princeton, N. J.: Princeton Univ. Press 1916
Durelli, Augusto J. *Liberation de la Liberté*. Montreal: Editions de l'Arbre 1944
Federation Internationale des Societies de Philosophie. *Enquête sur la Liberté*. Paris: Hermann 1953
Fellman, David. *The Limits of Freedom*. New Brunswick, N.J.: Rutgers Univ. Press 1959
Fromm, Erich. *Escape from Freedom*. N.Y.: Farrar & Rinehart 1951
    "        "      *The Fear of Freedom*. London: Paul, Trench, Trubner 1942
Ginzburg, Benjamin. *Rededication to Freedom*. N.Y.: Simon & Schuster 1959
Griffin, Alan. F. *Freedom, American Style*. N.Y.: Holt 1940
Grodzins, Morton. *The Loyal and the Disloyal*. Chicago: Univ. of Chicago Press 1956
Harper, F. A. *Liberty: A Path to Its Recovery*. Irvington-on-Hudson, N.Y.: Foundation for Economic Education 1949
Hook, Sidney. *Heresy, Yes—, Conspiracy, No*. N.Y.: John Day 1953
Hoover, Calvin B. *The Economy, Liberty and the State*. N.Y.: Twentieth Century Fund 1959
Huxley, Aldous. *Science, Liberty and Peace*. N.Y.: Fellowship Publications 1946
Joad, C. E. M. *Liberty Today*. N.Y.: Dutton 1935
Kallen, Horace M., Ed. *Freedom in the Modern World*. N.Y.: Coward McCann 1928
Kallen, Horace M. *The Liberal Spirit*. Ithaca, N.Y.: Cornell Univ. Press 1948
Konvitz, Milton R. & Hook, Sidney, Eds. *Freedom and Experience*. Ithaca, N.Y.: Cornell Univ. Press 1947
Lamont, Corliss. *Freedom is as Freedom Does*. N.Y.: Horizon Press 1956
LaMott, Robert L. *The Conservation of Freedom*. N.Y.: Exposition Press 1949
Laski, Harold J. *Liberty*, in the Encyclopedia of the Social Sciences
    "         "    *Liberty in the Modern State*. London: Faber & Faber 1930
Lasswell, Harold D. *National Security and Individual Freedom*. N.Y.: McGraw Hill 1951
Lauterpacht, H. *International Law and Human Rights*. N.Y.: Praeger 1950
LeFevre, Louis. *Liberty and Restraint*. N.Y.: Knopf 1926
Lieber, Francis. *On Civil Liberty and Self-Government*. Philadelphia: Lippincott 1880
Logan, George B. Jr. *Liberty in the Modern World*. Chapel Hill: Univ. of North Carolina Press 1928
MacIver, Robert M. *Academic Freedom in Our Time*. N.Y.: Columbia Univ. Press 1955

McKeon, Richard. *Freedom and History.* N.Y.: Noonday Press 1952
MacMurray, John. *Conditions of Freedom.* Toronto: Ryerson Press 1949
   "    "    *Freedom in the Modern World,* N.Y.: Appleton 1934
McWilliams, Carey. *Witch Hunt.* Boston: Little, Brown 1950
Mannheim, Karl. *Freedom, Power and Democratic Planning.* N.Y.: Oxford Univ. Press 1950
Maritain, Jacques. *Freedom in the Modern World.* London: Sheed & Ward, 1935
Mill, John Stuart. *On Liberty.* Boston: Ticknor & Fields 1865
   "    "    "    *On Social Freedom.* N.Y.: Columbia Univ. Press 1941
   "    "    "    *Prefaces to Liberty.* Boston: Beacon Press 1959
Miller, John C. *Crisis in Freedom.* Boston: Little, Brown 1952
Milton, John. *Areopagitica.* London: Dent 1955
Muller, Herbert J. *Issues of Freedom.* N.Y.: Harper 1960
Nesbit, Robert A. *The Quest for Community.* N.Y.: Oxford Univ. Press 1953
O'Brien, John Lord. *National Security and Individual Freedom.* Cambridge: Harvard Univ. Press 1955
Palmer, George H. *The Problem of Freedom.* Boston: Houghton Mifflin 1911
Rogge, O. John. *Our Vanishing Civil Liberties.* N.Y.: Gaer 1949
Rossiter, Clinton. *Seed-Time of the Republic: The Origin of the American Tradition of Political Liberty.* N.Y.: Harcourt, Brace 1953
Russell, Bertrand. *Authority and the Individual.* N. Y.: Simon & Schuster 1949
Russell, Bertrand. *Freedom and Organization.* London: Allen & Unwin 1934
Salvadori, Massimo. *The Economics of Freedom.* N.Y.: Doubleday 1959
Scherger, George L. *The Evolution of Modern Liberty.* N.Y.: Longmans Green 1904
Shotwell, James T. *The Long Way to Freedom.* Indianapolis: Bobbs-Merrill 1960
Spencer, Herbert. *The Man Versus the State.* London: Williams & Norgate 1907
Steiner, Rudolph. *Philosophy of Freedom.* N.Y.: Putnam 1916
Stouffer, Samuel A. *Communism, Conformity and Civil Liberties.* Garden City, N.Y.: Doubleday 1955
Streit, Clarence K. *Freedom Against Itself.* N.Y.: Harper 1955
Wallich, Henry C. *The Cost of Freedom.* N.Y.: Harper 1960
Wishey, Bernard. *Preface to Liberty: Selected Writings of John Stuart Mill.* Boston: Beacon Press 1959
Zilliacus, K. *A New Birth of Freedom?* N.Y.: Monthly Review Press 1958

# INDEX

Aggression in "free world," 74
American way, as conformity, 56
Anti-communism in "free world," 80
Armed force in the power age, 160
Authoritarianism in "free world," 80
Authority and freedom, 5

Belief, freedom of, 37
Belonging and freedom, 7
Business domination, 165
Business freedoms, 165
Business, as an institution, 164

Capitalism and socialism compared, 186
Change frustrates freedom, 47
Choice and freedom, 4
Civil rights, 40
Civil war and freedom, 12
Collective effort, advantage of, 9
Colonialism and freedom, 20
Common interests and individual interests, 10
Competition and freedom, 12
Conformity, and compulsion, 53; and freedom, 11, 51; and group survival, 53; and social change, 56; and social pressures, 55; defined, 51; involves social pressures, 51; limits freedom, 51; pattern of, 52; replaces freedom, 54
Corporate business enterprise as imperialism, 170
Corruption, freedom for, 69

Crisis in free world, 79
Culture traits and conformity, 53

Demands for freedom, 35
Destruction and freedom, 14
Disasters and freedom, 48
Disease limits freedom, 46

Economic freedom, 41; and the "free world," 59
Economic surplus and freedom, 20
Emergencies, and freedom, 48; and social transition, 175
Ends of freedom, 28
Equilibrium and freedom, 7
Eternal vigilance and freedom, 27
Expansion and overhead costs, 168
Experiments with freedom, 82
Expression, freedom of, 38
External causes and freedom, 5

Flight from freedom, 71
Free enterprise, and modern business, 41; and monopoly, 66; as menace, 66; as social force, 19; in West, 19; on the frontier, 154
"Free world," a threat to peace, 77; aggression of, 74; and imperialism, 168; and monopoly capitalism, 75; and private enterprise, 74; anticommunist ideology of, 80; crisis in, 79; decline of, 76; despotism in, 84; freedom in, 57, 73; imperialism in, 58; militarism in, 78; or-

199

ganization of, 81; pattern of, 78

Freedom, a consequence of group activity, 27; a good in itself, 28; a relationship, 13; a social product, 25; an associational term, 138; an end in itself, 28, 56; an incomplete term, 29, 140; and business enterprise, 163; and civil war, 12; and colonialism, 20, 61; and conformity, 11, 51; and destruction, 29; and discrimination, 61; and emergency, 49, 137; and Europeanization, 21; and gregariousness, 156; and group priority, 158; and human nature, 24; and its opposites, 14, 15, 140; and liberty, 139; and national sovereignty, 159; and necessity, 44; and opportunity, 19; and physical incapacity, 117; and polarity, 13; and related ideas, 14; and responsibility, 136, 188; and restraint, 4, 5; and social adjustments, 120; and social transition, 175; and socialist construction, 186; and solidarity, 156; and status quo, 11; and the rule of reason, 121; and wagery, 62; as a social force, 22; as association, 14; as absence of restraint, 14; as attitude, 4; as cause, 18; as consequence, 23; as imperialist propaganda, 169; as instrument, 29; as means, 29; as normal function, 7; as relationship, 138; as separateness, 7; becomes a menace, 65; comes first, 19, 117, 152; complexity of, 139; consequences of, 192; defined, 3 ff.; demands for, 35; divisive nature of, 12; evaluation of, 192; experiments with, 82; fear of, 72; for business, 164, 165; for chattel slaves, 60; for criminals, 64; for groups, 43; for minorities, 169; for small enterprises, 60; for unearned income, 67; for war-making, 71; in bourgeois society, 163; in conflict situations, 125; in idea and action, 190; in inten-

tional communities, 86; in organized society, 49; in modern history, 17; in the "free world," 73; in the power age state, 122; in western civilization, 19, 161; joys of, 55; leads to imperialism, 167; limited by personality, 117; man-made, 24; menace of, 64; neutrality of, 30; not a good in itself, 140; not an abstraction, 140; on the frontier, 87; promise of, 56; relativity of, 16, 132; restraint and social transition, 173; to be alone, 40; to corrupt, 68; to destroy, 70; to exploit, 67; to think, 37; to waste, 67; under law, 127; within authority, 125; varies with time and place, 134

Freedom age, 26

Freedom century, 89; breakdown of, 90

Freedom demands, and conflict, 12; multiplicity of, 35

Freedom from desire, 4

Freedom in theory, restraint in practise, 133

Freedom is experimental, 90

Freedom is not enough, 193

Freedom-necessity opposition, 45, 50

Freedom, of belief, 37; of expression, 38; of movement, 35

Freedom priority, 153

Freedom-restraint, balance of, 15; in the power age, 146; in social history, 16, 22; opposition of, 16; shifts of, 16

Freedoms increase in number, 44

General social crisis, dilemma of, 171

General welfare and freedom, 10

Get-rich-quick, as incentive, 21

Golden Mean and choice, 8

Good life, ingredients of, 121; possibilities of, 149

Gregariousness and human nature, 156

Group freedom, 43; and individual subjugation, 162; and power pol-